HAUNTED CREEDE

HAUNTED CREEDE

KANDRA PAYNE

Haunted
America

Published by Haunted America
A Division of The History Press
Charleston, SC
www.historypress.com

First published 2020

Manufactured in the United States

ISBN 9781467144551

Library of Congress Control Number: 2020938431

Notice: The information in this book is true and complete to the best of our knowledge. It is offered without guarantee on the part of the author or The History Press. The author and The History Press disclaim all liability in connection with the use of this book.

This book is dedicated to Maddie, who loves both Creede and a good ghost story just as much as I do. If it happens to be a Creede ghost story, all the better.

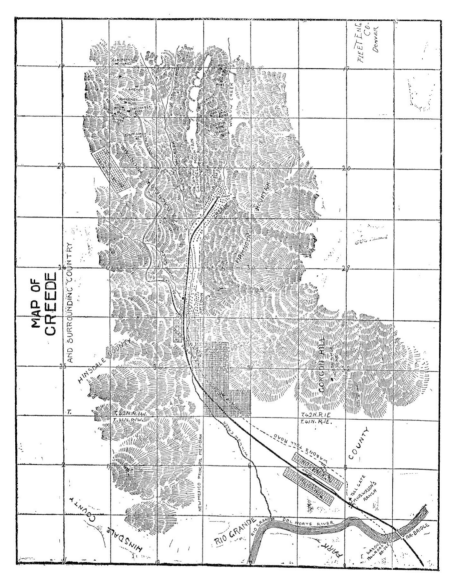

An 1892 map of Creede and surrounding country. *From the* Creede Candle, *Colorado Historic Newspapers online.*

CONTENTS

FOREWORD

The now tiny (population approximately three hundred) town of Creede where Kandra Payne was raised holds an outsized history of boom, bust and rebirth. The last great silver boomtown in Colorado, the Creede mining district once boasted approximately ten thousand residents. Saloons, gambling halls and brothels were ubiquitous as miners sought escape from their dreary and backbreaking daily labor. As newspaperman Cy Warman noted in 1892, "It's day all day in the daytime and there is no night in Creede." Notorious characters such as Calamity Jane, Bat Masterson, Soapy Smith and Poker Alice all resided or visited Creede during its brief heyday. Another notable resident, Bob Ford, the assassin of Jesse James, was gunned down in his Creede saloon in 1892, ten years after killing James. By any measure, Creede was an iconic mining boom town and an important contributor to what made the Wild West wild.

A relative newcomer to Creede, compared to Kandra, I first visited in 1992, quickly fell in love with the area and the community and subsequently built a home, where I have resided full time since 2004. Always something of a history buff, I was immediately engrossed by Creede's boisterous origins and soon became involved with the Creede Historical Society, where I conduct oral history interviews with local old-timers and chair the museum committee, which runs the historical museum housed in the 1893 Denver and Rio Grande Railroad Depot.

Like most everyone in Creede, I had heard of Tom Payne, a long-time local miner with a legendary history of state and national mining competition championships. I hadn't met his daughter, Kandra, however, until she approached me a few years ago about the possibility of conducting local ghost tours and using our depot museum as the tours' start and endpoints. Although I was familiar with ghost tours in cities such as New Orleans, where I lived for several years, I was, to put it mildly, a paranormal skeptic. In addition, I frankly didn't believe ghost tours would find many takers in Creede. My oral history interviews had uncovered a few "ghostly" tales as well as reports of inexplicable goings-on in the mines, generally attributed to the mythical Tommy Knockers of mining folklore. Still, it didn't seem like much to build a tour around. Kandra convinced me, however, that she had accumulated an abundance and we scheduled a couple of tours to see what would happen. Quite surprisingly (to me at least), the tours were an instant hit, with more willing patrons than our small museum could accommodate. Based on this initial success, the tours became a highly popular weekly event throughout the summer season and a welcome source of revenue for the Creede Historical Society.

Kandra's tours are not merely entertaining, they add significant new insights and discoveries to the Creede area historical record. Kandra's compelling stories are based on her extensive research and deserve the protection and preservation provided by publication. I was, therefore, delighted when Kandra told me she was planning a book based on her stories. I thank her for that important historical contribution and for helping me look just a bit more skeptically at my paranormal skepticism.

—Jim Loud, Museum Committee Chair, Creede Historical Society

PREFACE

Several years ago, I took a trip with my husband, Scott, to Victoria, British Columbia. While strolling through the streets, we saw a sign advertising a ghost tour. I begged him to go along with me, and he, being a paranormal skeptic, protested loud and long but finally gave in to my enthusiastic cajoling. At the end of our tour, he turned to me and thanked me for persuading him to go. Pleasantly surprised to have learned so much local history on this one-hour walk and having seen some pretty spectacular places that we'd otherwise have missed, he had loved the tour. The spooky tales expertly told by our guide had added an immediateness to the history, had brought Victoria's past to life. Later that night, Scott told me, "This kind of tour would work well in Creede, and you already know all the ghost stories!" The idea germinated, and I became convinced that he was right. It became one of my dreams to share Creede's rich history by creating its very own ghost tour. In 2017, as Creede prepared for its 125th anniversary, the time was right to put the tour into action. The Creede Ghost Tour became part of that anniversary weekend celebration and enjoyed much success. Ever since that first summer, the ghost tour has shared Creede's history with hundreds of people. This book grew from the requests of several tour guests to see these stories in writing. I began collecting these Creede ghost stories as a child. My collection and fascination with history grew as I did, always immensely proud to be from this charming and unique little mountain town with its boomtown beginnings and claims of being one of the wildest places in the Wild West. Putting my collection in writing has been a labor of

Businesses along Cliff Street in Jimtown (now Creede) prior to the fire of June 5, 1892, including Creede Undertaking & Embalming. Note the advertisement hung from high on the cliffs above and the large electric streetlight in the left foreground. *Ken Wyley Collection, Creede Historical Society Archives.*

love. I liken it to piecing together a jigsaw puzzle of historic facts and eerie stories, tracing personages through newspaper archives, learning who these women and men were, what they did, how they came to live in Creede, what their contributions were to the boomtown they found themselves in, and why they might still remain here in spectral form. At times, I felt the ghosts reaching out to me, guiding my research, and I hope that in some small way, I can return the favor. There is a saying that every person dies two deaths, one being corporeal and the second and final being the last time the person's name is spoken aloud. It is my hope that by sharing these stories and speaking these names, I'm doing my part in keeping both their memory and history itself alive.

ACKNOWLEDGEMENTS

I'd like to thank my family, first and foremost, for listening to me talk endlessly about Creede's history and ghosts as I researched, prepared and wrote first the ghost tour and then this collection of tales. Thank you to Scott, Maddie, Mom, Dad, Jennie Kay, Thomas, Hunter, Allison and Kambrie for your love, unwavering support and patience.

To Vern Tonkin, who proofread meticulously and provided invaluable feedback, your brilliance and commitment are appreciated more than you can possibly imagine.

Jim Loud and David Clark did their share of wordsmithing, believing in and supporting this project whole-heartedly from its inception. I am lucky beyond measure to have you both on my team.

Starr Pearson and Shirrae Fazio provided the day-to-day encouragement that kept this project on the rails even when the going got tough. My gratitude is immense.

Johanna Gray spent hours and hours with me perusing the Creede Historical Society's library in search of ghosts. Thank you for your dedication and for making the research so much fun.

Thank you to Jan Jacobs, Bob Seago and Allison Quiller, who helped me locate the images in the Creede Historical Society's archive that would bring these stories to life. Special thanks to Bob, who took the time to snap a few shots especially for this book.

My gratitude to John Gary Brown and Christy Brandt is immeasurable. They supported the idea of the ghost tour from the beginning, helped bring the tour to life and then generously allowed me access to their amazing collection of photographs for this book.

Thanks to Susan Madrid and Catherine Kim, who sold ghost tour tickets, talked it up, and never let me give up on the tour or the book.

And finally, to all the amazing people who trusted me enough to share their personal ghostly encounters, I thank you from the bottom of my heart.

An early funeral on Creede's boot hill. Note the snow on the ground, possibly making this the funeral of "Gambler Joe" Simmons (March 1892). *John Gary Brown Collection.*

A burro nurses her foal on Creede's Main Street, date unknown. *John Gary Brown Collection.*

The Rise and Fall of Creede

A thousand burdened burros filled
    The narrow, winding, wriggling trail.
A hundred settlers came to build,
    Each day, new houses in the vale.
A hundred gamblers came to feed
On these same settlers—this was Creede.

Slanting Annie, Gambler Joe,
    And Robert Ford; old Olio—
Or Soapy Smith, as he was known—
    Ran games peculiarly their own,
And everything was open wide
And men drank absinthe on the side.

And now the Faro Bank is closed,
    And Mr. Faro's gone away
To seek new fields, it is supposed,
    Most verdant fields. The gamblers say
The man who worked the shell and ball
Has gone back to the Capitol.

The winter winds blow bleak and chill
    The quaking, quivering aspen waves
About the summit of the hill—
    Above the unrecorded graves.
Where half abandoned burros feed
And coyotes call—and this is Creede.

Lone graves! whose headboards bear no name
    Whose silent owners lived like brutes.
And died as doggedly, but game;
    And most of them died in their boots.
We find among the unwrit names
The man who murdered Jesse James.

We saw him murdered, saw him fall,
  And saw his mad assassin gloat
Above him; heard his moans and all
  And saw the shot holes in his throat.
And men moved on and gave no heed
To life or death—and this is Creede.

Slanting Annie, Gambler Joe,
  And Missouri Bob are sleeping there,
But Slippery, sly old Olio,
  Who seems to shun the golden stair,
Has turned his time to loftier tricks—
He's doing Denver politics.

—Cy Warman, published in the Silverton Standard, *November 26, 1892*

INTRODUCTION

How are we to account for the strange human craving for the pleasure of feeling afraid which is so much involved in our love of ghost stories?
—Virginia Woolf

Before there was the town of Creede, the Ute Indians laid claim to this region. Their summer hunting grounds were here, and it was land worth protecting. In the mid-1800s, when settlers began venturing farther and farther into the Indian territories, these Utes did not stand idly by. One old story passed along over the decades says that the Utes would wait atop the cliffs that tower over both sides of what is now Wagon Wheel Gap and ambush any wagon that dared to enter through the cut. It is said that they brutally defended that entrance, and once these encroaching settlers were killed, they were scalped and the scalps then strung on a long rope with a wagon wheel dangling from the center. This rope was then stretched over the gap at its narrowest opening and suspended between the two cliffs, displaying a clear and gruesome warning to anyone else who might happen along this same path. While there are other stories, this is the darkest and most gruesome version of how Wagon Wheel Gap got its name.[1]

I challenge you to drive through the gap now without looking for that narrow opening where the Utes might have strung a rope. Once I learned that story, I was unable able to forget it. That stretch of road has always been unsettling to me, as a matter of fact. As a child, and my parents can attest to this, I would hide on the floor in the back of the car when we turned the

Stage stop at Wagon Wheel Gap, date unknown. *John Gary Brown Collection.*

corner and approached the gap on our way home from my grandparents' house in South Fork. Mostly this occurred when we traveled the road at night, but I was known to cower in the back even on daytime trips. It was the mountain I feared—the mountain that rose like a giant from the earth, hulking shoulders and head pushing up from beyond the river. I knew that this mountain was a monster and that one day he would continue to rise; his arms would extend, fists pounding, and crush our car and anything else that might be in his way. Even as I grew older and put these childhood fears behind me, I could not escape a shudder when passing through the gap and within reach of the "monster mountain." The fear was almost primeval, irrational and, for me, inescapable.

When I first learned of the dark and bloody tale regarding the stretch of road leading in to Creede, I began to wonder if it was the history itself, the impressions and ghosts left behind that I sensed as a child trembling there in the back of our Ford Galaxy as we drove through Wagon Wheel Gap. Whatever the reason, the terror was real, and it seems a fitting way to open my collection of ghost stories. For there is something strangely delicious about feeling scared when we hear and read about ghosts. Perhaps it's because it opens our minds to new, unseen possibilities and potential. In this fear lives hope—hope that there is something beyond what we know and experience in our everyday life, hope that there is an afterlife, hope that we will someday see our deceased loved ones again.

Prospectors were looking for minerals in the San Juan Mountains around Creede as early as 1860, but it wasn't until the early 1870s that the first mines were established in the San Juan range.[2] This was a time in the West when native peoples were being moved from their lands either forcibly or through treaties with the government. The Utes who used the area around Creede as valuable hunting grounds had already been moved to a reservation encompassing nearly a third of western Colorado, but mineral-rich Creede was located on their lands and the government could see that they could not prevent incursions into Ute territory by prospectors. It was the Brunot Agreement in 1873 that carved out a portion of the San Juan Mountains from the Ute reservation and made it possible for the prospectors to establish permanent mines and settlements in search of mineral deposits while allowing the Ute to maintain hunting rights on the land.[3] A few scattered mining claims were staked in the area that is now Creede in the 1870s, but it would not be until 1889 that Nicholas C. Creede would wander up East Willow Canyon and discover the claim that would start the last big silver boom our nation would see. The camp that sprang up and eventually bore the name Creede grew steadily in its original location at the junction of East and West Willow Creek and then boomed with a vengeance once Nicholas Creede sold the Holy Moses claim for $70,000 in 1890.[4] Though the settlement was originally called Willow, miners voted to change the name to Creede in honor of the hardworking and fortunate prospector. Creede became a household name to many across the country, and everyone wanted to go to Creede and strike it rich. It wasn't just miners and prospectors who populated the booming camp; there were merchants, gamblers, dance hall girls and a large array of all sorts of characters. The population exploded; at the height of the boom, there were ten thousand people living in the district.[5] The tiny Creede Camp which was situated between the steep walls of the canyon spread to the south, and the narrow area of the canyon downstream became Stringtown. At the southern end, where the canyon opened up and there was more room for building, Jimtown sprang into being. Eventually all of this would be called Creede, but not before a raging fire would burn most of Jimtown's business district to the ground on June 5, 1892. After the fire, much of Creede was rebuilt, this time with more fire-resistant brick, but the town of Creede would never again see the glory of those boom days. The 1893 repeal of the Sherman Silver Purchase Act

Main Street, Creede, Colorado, December 1942. *Library of Congress; photograph by Andreas Feininger.*

dramatically lowered the price of silver, closing many of Creede's mines and leading to a drastic decline in population. Despite its hardships, the town of Creede would never be completely abandoned or become a ghost town, although many ghosts may call Creede home.

Between the pages of this book you will find the stories of several of Creede's earliest residents and tales of their ghosts. You will meet a ghost who balks at any mention of disturbing his clandestine resting place, one who wanders in search of his corporeal remains, another that's still trying to make moonshine, a widow who weeps for her lost love, a helpful spirit, one who plays the violin, and an angry entity with which you don't want to tangle. My hope is that these stories will spark wonder as well as fear and that you will be inspired to further explore Creede's fascinating history. Stoke your fire, pull up a chair, nestle in with a cup of hot cocoa and read on to discover the captivating secrets of Haunted Creede. Turn the page when you are ready, and we will travel back to the 1870s down the old stagecoach route through Wagon Wheel Gap and up the Rio Grande to the stage stop at San Juan City to meet our first ghost.

1

WHAT LIES BENEATH

*A world in which there are monsters, and ghosts,
and things that want to steal your heart is a world in which there are angels,
and dreams and a world in which there is hope.*
——*Neil Gaiman*

If one is searching for ghosts, it stands to reason that you might start by looking at the oldest house in the region. For Creede, that would be an old stagecoach stop that predates the town by almost twenty years. This rustic yet grand log and stone home sits about eighteen miles upriver in a lovely meadow next to a rushing creek at the foot of Bristol Head Mountain. In the 1870s, before Creede ever existed, the Barlow and Sanderson Stagecoach Line ran through the area delivering passengers, goods and mail between Del Norte, Lake City and Silverton. There were stagecoach stops about every ten miles along this route, the two nearest the current site of Creede being Wagon Wheel Gap and Antelope Springs, also called Alden's Junction (currently Broken Arrow Ranch), where the stage line split, one route heading to Silverton the other to Lake City.[6] About six miles farther upriver was another stage stop at what was then called Antelope Park. Antelope Park had two stops essentially, the first being at San Juan City (currently Freemon's Ranch) and the second a few miles down the road at Galloway's (currently San Juan Ranch). The San Juan City stop was an oasis along the dusty mountain line for food and lodging, while the Galloway stop dealt primarily with freight and stock handling.[7] The stop at San Juan City originally held the post office and was

An early picture of the stage stop, post office and lodging built by Clarence and Ada "Dolly" Brooks long before Creede was on the map. *Creede Historical Society Archives.*

built by Clarence W. Brooks and his young bride, Ada or "Dolly," around 1875 (although some sources date its construction as early as 1866).[8] Still standing and in use, the large ranch house at Freemon's Guest Ranch is thought to be the oldest building in the upper Rio Grande area. This stage stop at San Juan City was described in a September 1875 article detailing the journey from Wagon Wheel Gap to Silverton:

> *C.W. Brooks has erected a substantial stone building…where a post office has been established and supplied with semi-weekly mail from Del Norte. For charming scenery, excellent trout fishing, grass and water, this surpasses any place within my knowledge. Its altitude is 9,000 feet.…Those who have occasion to test Mr. and Mrs. Brooks hospitality will not regret it. Many of the comforts and conveniences of well-established and older stations are to be met with here.[9]*

Swedish-born Dolly was only seventeen when she married Clarence Brooks, and together they ran the roadhouse and post office at San Juan City. The stories passed down by the old-timers describe her as a "red-light" or dance hall girl who was also quite a beauty.[10] The buxom Dolly was said to refer to herself as a perfect "36" and, although married, apparently entertained clientele in the barroom by dancing on the tables.[11]

Sometime in the late 1870s, a baby girl was born to Clarence and Dolly. They named the baby Hermione, but she did not live long. She is thought

Above: Stage stop at Wagon Wheel Gap, date unknown. *John Gary Brown Collection.*

Right: Flamboyant cowboy James L. Wing, second husband of Dolly Brooks. *Creede Historical Society Archives.*

to be buried in a small grave near the San Juan City site. In the early 1880s, the pair divorced and went their separate ways. At the time, it was common for a couple's business and property to be put in the wife's name to avoid legal and financial issues, and this was the case with the Brooks.[12] When they split, Dolly got the roadhouse and property at San Juan City. Clarence left the area and did not return, while Dolly continued to run things at the stage stop and ranch. In 1885, at the age of twenty-six, Dolly fell in love and married a "flamboyant cowboy" named James L. Wing.[13] Dolly delivered a baby boy, Edelbert W. Wing, in March 1887, but again, the baby did not live long. It is supposed that this baby is also buried in the small grave site with baby Hermione. Six months later, in September 1887, Dolly herself died or disappeared, depending on the source. Some speculate that she perished from a broken heart after losing two babies; others say she tired of James Wing and "flew the coop" with a former beau.[14] One old-timer reports that at the time, many people suspected James Wing of poisoning Dolly to gain control of her considerable assets. They thought James had possibly concocted the tale of Dolly abandoning him as a cover story for having done away with her himself. This theory went further, venturing that James used rat poison to kill her, as a receipt turned up around that time for a poison called Rough on Rats. It had been purchased for fifteen cents from a pharmacy over the mountain in Lake City.[15] A quick search of historical newspapers in the 1880s turned up many ads for the rat poison. Composed of arsenic and a small amount of coal for color, and readily available at most pharmacies, it was a popular product. There was even an advertising ditty about Rough on Rats (sung to the tune of "Little Brown Jug"):

Squalling children, scolding wife,
Were not the pest of my poor life;
Where'er I lived, in house or flats,
My plague has been those horrid Rats.
They ate our meat, our bread and shoes,
We could not have a quiet snooze;
One day my wife did chance to dose,
They pinned my baby by the nose.

CHORUS.
R-r-rats! Rats! Rats! Rough on Rats!
Hang your dog and drown your cats;
We give a plan for every man
To clear his house with ROUGH ON RATS.[16]

Rough on Rats advertisement, 1887.
*Public domain, www.flickr.com/photos/
internetarchivebookimages/14598199427.*

The product was both popular and *dangerous*. Several accounts of suicides, accidental poisonings, mysterious deaths and, of course, murders involving Rough on Rats were reported in a variety of sources. Clearly, James Wing could have had a legitimate use for rat poison to control the vermin on the ranch, but we may never know to what purpose that arsenic was used. Whether Dolly flew the coop, was indeed poisoned or simply died of a broken heart, some believe she is buried with her two babies in the grave site that is now a part of San Juan Ranch.

There are several other colorful tales about the old ranch house, but perhaps the most intriguing is an account that takes place in the barroom of that old stage stop. Given the history presented, one might assume the ghostly story to follow will center on the spirit of Dolly Brooks Wing. It does not, but Dolly very well may have been around and possibly even involved in the events leading up to the haunting. Legend has it that there was once a gun duel in the saloon at the stage stop and that the skeletal remains of the man who was not quick on the draw lie to this day under the floorboards of what is now the recreation room at Freemon's Guest Ranch.

In 1968, when Ken Ellison and his family first purchased and moved on to Freemon's Guest Ranch, they began to hear stories from some of the old-timers who lived nearby: "You know there's a body buried under your floor there, right?" asked Charles Dabney. Ken replied that he did not and didn't think too much about it until he heard the same story in more detail from John LaFont, a Creede native, local historian and author.

John began by explaining that the house had once been a stagecoach stop with a saloon and boardinghouse. Many a weary traveler passed through the doors of the saloon in those days, and the story went that one night a man came in alone and began drinking. Growing surlier the more he drank, this man appeared to be "on the shoot," or itching for a fight. He finally riled another patron enough to rise from his barstool and throw the first punch. A terrible fight ensued, ending in a gun duel and

The oldest building in the Upper Rio Grande area, once a stage stop, is still in use as the ranch house, office and recreation room at Freemon's Guest Ranch. *Photograph by Ed Cannon.*

leaving the lone traveler lying dead on the dirt floor of the saloon. At that point, the bartender and San Juan City locals gathered around the body to discuss what should be done. There was no law enforcement for miles around, and did they really want to implicate one of their own in this man's death? If they took the body outside to bury it, somebody might see, and suspicions would be aroused. They decided to take no chances, and instead of sending for the law, they sent to the barn for a shovel. A deep hole was dug right there in the dirt floor of the saloon, and the lifeless traveler was buried near where he had fallen. Another version of this story has them throwing the lone traveler into the small root cellar, filling it in with a shovel and then covering the entrance to the cellar with a trunk until a wooden plank floor could be installed.

Ken listened with interest to the story but soon forgot about it as he returned to the challenging business of running the ranch. The old story was nearly forgotten entirely until one evening when the topic of ghost stories came up at the dinner table. Ken recounted the story of the body buried in what was now the ranch's recreation room. His daughter Starr was shocked, as anyone might be to learn that it is supposed that a dead man is buried under the floor of your home. She decided that she really needed to know

The old barn and hay loft at Freemon's Guest Ranch. *Author collection.*

if the story was true. Could they remove the wooden plank floor and begin digging in search of this body? If found, perhaps they could give the man a proper burial? It was all just dinnertime chatter, and they laughed about what may or may not lie under those floorboards.

They were not laughing later that night though when the entire family was roused from their beds as the old log house began to shake as if there were an earthquake. A terrible booming echoed through the rooms. It lasted a few moments and then stopped. Puzzled and anxious. the family returned to their beds. In the morning. they asked those who had been sleeping in other cabins on the ranch if they too had experienced the horrible shaking and booming of the previous evening. No one in the vicinity or beyond had heard or felt a thing. Life on the ranch went on as usual.

The author's father and Elks member, Tom Payne, leans against the bar at the Creede Elks Lodge, BPOE No. 506. *Author collection.*

Several months later, Starr again raised the subject of searching for the body under the floorboards. On that very evening, the shaking and reverberating booms returned to haunt the Ellisons in the middle of the night. The next morning at breakfast, it was decided that the man buried under the floorboards was trying to communicate with them and his message was clear: He did not want anyone to look for him or dig him up, and he certainly did not want to be moved from his resting place. The topic is now never discussed in the ranch house, and things have remained peaceful ever since.

The saloon at the San Juan City stage stop, later to be called the Texas Club, once had an ornately carved back bar where the liquor bottles were stored. This back bar was sold to the Creede Elks Lodge and brought into Creede sometime in the early 1900s. You can get a look at it in the bar and lounge area of the Elks Lodge, where it is still in service to this day. So the next time you happen to be up in the Creede Elks Lodge, saddle on up to that timeworn bar. There is some evidence that Creede's most infamous resident, Bob Ford, may have been shot over this very bar, so raise a glass in his memory. Then take a moment to look deep into the mirror behind the bar; that back bar was once about eighteen miles upriver, and according to some old-timers, it reflected from this very glass a vicious bar fight, the clandestine burial of a dead man, and the beautiful face of Dolly Brooks Wing.

2

THE GHOST OF McGINTY

*Skeptics don't have faith in the local ghost descriptions, but other people swear,
in fact, that bloodcurdling things are going on in Creede during the night.
A semi decomposed human dead body has supposedly been noticed on
numerous instances trying to find a bag on the water's edge of
Lower Homestake Tailings Pond. McGinty no doubt.* [17]

These ominous lines appear in an article titled "Creede Hauntings, Are You Frightened?" printed by the *Mineral County Miner* in October 2009. But who (or what) is McGinty, and why would this corpse-like specter skulk about the lower end of Creede? To answer these questions, we need to step back in time to February 1892, the very height of Creede's boom.

One of the strangest and most fascinating tales to come from the days of Creede's boom is that of Soapy Smith and his petrified man. It illustrates the circus-like atmosphere that prevailed in the camp's early days and spotlights Soapy as the undisputed ringmaster. This tale involves the supposedly petrified body of a man being "discovered" by a gentleman named J.J. Dore (supposed by many to have been an associate of Soapy Smith) and dug up from the banks of Farmers Creek, brought into camp and put on display. A person could view this petrification, dubbed McGinty by the *Creede Candle*, for the low price of twenty-five cents (about seven dollars in today's currency). [18] Of course, the real money was to be made from the captive audiences standing in line, rife for the picking as Soapy or one of his compatriots ran their shell games and other cons outside. Some historians claim that Creede's "petrified man" was made of cement and that the gig was up when the concrete began to disintegrate and flake away.[19] Soapy Smith's own great-grandson, a writer and historian himself, has a different and quite compelling theory of his own regarding the origins of the petrified man. He believes the petrified man might very well have been a gambler who caused some trouble in Soapy's Orleans Club one winter night in February 1892. The young gambler, known as the Louisiana Kid, according to Smith's theory, was then killed by the Soap Gang, sent away for preservation and finally returned to Creede and put on exhibit as the morbid sideshow-like attraction—the petrified man.[20] A more detailed account of his demise is discussed later in this chapter.

Soapy Smith arrived in Creede with his Soap Gang sometime during the winter of 1891–92. Anti-gambling legislation had been passed in Denver, and several large gambling houses and operators were hightailing it out of there. With its "wondrous wealth untold" as Cy Warman put it, and lack of law enforcement, the Creede Camp presented a perfect opportunity for these men to set up shop, run their games and swindle the masses. Soapy's most famous con, unique to him and the one for which he earned his nickname went something like this:

> On a busy street corner near the depot, dark-eyed and dapper Smith set up a little folding table on which he piled several dozen cakes of ordinary toilet soap and squares of bright blue wrapping paper. While he entertained a curious crowd with a fine repertoire of ballads and a line of snappy patter, he twisted $10.00, $20.00 and even a few $100.00 bills around the cakes of soap before wrapping them in blue squares. He then tossed the packages carelessly into a pile on the table and offered them to the suckers at only $5.00 each.
>
> An associate of the con man would be the first buyer, and sure enough he would find a $100.00 bill which he flashed to the crowd. That started the landslide! Anxious buyers piled up around the table and pushed $5.00 bills into Smith's face almost faster than he could grab them. Few got more than a nickel cake of soap. With nimble-fingered Smith handling the soap and the money, they had little chance.[21]

Built in early 1892, Soapy's saloon and gambling hall in Creede was called the Orleans Club, and it sat in a prominent spot on Creede Avenue in Jimtown. This location is just north of where the Creede Repertory Theatre stands today.[22] Among the wildest spots on the raucous street,

The busy intersection of Creede Avenue (now Main Street) and Wall Street, circa 1891–92. The tent in the lower right is thought by some to have been where Soapy operated before his Orleans Club was completed. *John Gary Brown Collection.*

Jefferson "Soapy" Smith standing at the bar in a saloon in Skagway, Alaska, not long before his death in 1898. *Library of Congress.*

Soapy Smith's Orleans Club (*right*), flying the American flag, circa early 1892. Note the woodpile in the foreground, likely the hiding spot where the Louisiana Kid lay in wait before the famed gunfight with Joe Palmer. *Creede Historical Society Archives.*

it drew attention one night when a character called the Louisiana Kid raised havoc after losing a good deal of money on a bet. Thrown out of the Orleans Club by manager and Soap Gang member Joe Palmer, the Louisiana Kid waited for Palmer in the dark street outside the club. When Palmer later stepped out into the frigid night, a gunfight ensued. The *Creede Candle* reported it this way:

> There was a shooting affray in Jimtown last Thursday night. "Louisiana Kid," believing his rights had been trod upon in a social game of draw laid in wait for Manager Palmer of Jeff Smith's place and opened up his artillery when Palmer came out of the house. Palmer did some shooting on his own account. The Kid was wounded, but got away, and was last seen hitting the pike for the south. Palmer had both thumbs shot off and got a ball in the hip and a scratch on the head. For a while guns were kept hot in the camp, but no serious results are reported.[23]

The famous professional gambler Poker Alice Tubbs, who dealt faro across the street from the Orleans Club in Bob Ford's Exchange, gave her firsthand account of this same gunfight in an interview she did in 1927 with the *Saturday Evening Post*:

> I was returning to my little log cabin in Creede when suddenly, from both sides of me, shots began to spurt in the semidarkness of the little town. Vaguely I saw a man behind a woodpile and another opposite, each with a revolver and each pulling the trigger with intent to kill. I did the natural thing—I made for the first and nearest saloon, since saloons were about the most plentiful of business houses in the town. Steve Scribner's place was handiest, and while Steve tried to push the door closed to lock it I pushed as enthusiastically to get in, while the shooting went on behind me.
>
> "Let me in!" I shouted. "It's only Poker Alice!"
>
> There was nothing else, incidentally, for Scribner to do; I was jammed in the door by this time. Wilder and wilder the shooting became, suddenly to cease that the noise of exploding cartridges might give way to heightened wailing.
>
> "I'm a son of a gun!" said Steve Scribner beside me in the darkness. "is that one of those fellows who's just been shooting to kill? He's bawling like a baby!"
>
> The sound grew louder, accompanied by words:
>
> "Don't shoot anymore! Don't shoot anymore! You've knocked both my thumbs off!"

Then the battle, which had been intended a moment before as a struggle unto death, became quickly an affair of humor.

"Listen to the big baby cry!" shouted the man who had shot off his assailant's thumbs.

"Oh, what a baby!" echoed the spectators, flooding now from behind barricades and other selected spots of protection. The howling man, mourning the loss of his thumbs, found himself the owner of a new nickname. He was Baby Joe and Baby Joe he stayed as long as I can remember.[24]

Now if someone happens to get both thumbs shot off in a gunfight, I'd say they are entitled to a bit of crying, but apparently, people were a tougher lot and things were a bit different in Creede in 1892. Another eyewitness to this scrape gave an account that showed Joe Palmer in a more favorable light:

"In those days," said the man with the broad white hat, "Creede was a booming camp. You can make books on that. And it was a camp that it pleased an old timer to set foot in. Tenderfeet were not stacking up against the fellows then. It was a reminder of Deadwood and Leadville. It was reminiscence of forty-nine.

"But as I was saying, that fight that Joe Palmer made against the 'Orleans Kid' was as good and game a fight as a man ever saw….Down in Creede he ran a house for Jeff Smith. The Kid came in there one night and got noisy and abusive. The fact that he had killed four men didn't cut a figure with Joe, and he politely but firmly told him to get out. The Kid left sulkily, and we fellows at the tables watching the play between turns of the cards just took a flier, in our inner consciousness, that there'd be trouble before morning.

Joe stepped out of the place a little afterward. He was gone but a moment or two when we hear a shot. We sprang up from our chips, leaving our bets on the layout, and rushed outside. And there we saw a fight!

Palmer was standing in the middle of the street right under the electric light. In the bright glare he was the fairest of targets. The Kid was by the corner in the shadow of the stores. Both of them were blazing away at less than 30 paces. The Kid's second bullet struck Joe in the thumb of his pistol hand, and the gun fell to the ground. Joe picked it up with his left hand and went on shooting. Another bullet from The Kid struck Joe's left thumb, and the six shooter dropped again. We all thought Joe would run then for sure, because we couldn't see how he could ever cock his gun to keep up the fight. He stooped over, as cool as you please, grabbed his gun in his right hand and cocked it by rubbing it downward against his leg.

When the two men had used up all the cartridges and the fight was over, the Kid staggered away. He had lost. Four of Joe's six bullets had hit him."[25]

Did the Louisiana Kid lurch away from the gunfight mortally wounded by the bullets from Joe Palmer's six-shooter and die that freezing night under the starry Creede sky? Maybe. The *Creede Candle* does not tell us what might have been the result of his wounds, and since no paper ever reported the Kid's given name, it is impossible to follow up on his fate. Jeff Smith thinks the Louisiana Kid did die that night, and he believes that the Kid's body was later put on a train and sent away to be preserved, or "petrified."[26] The body of the petrified man would be dug up that April by J.J. Dore, only two months after that fateful gunfight. First displayed at Creede's Hotel Vaughn and later "purchased" by Soapy Smith and moved to the Orleans Club, McGinty proved a profitable venture for those who exhibited him.[27] After leaving Creede, Soapy took McGinty back to Denver to display there, later leasing him out to a variety of attractions and finally selling him in 1895 to a merchant in Washington State.[28]

Sylvester, a preserved human mummy who might well have been Soapy Smith's McGinty, is to this day on display in Washington State—along Seattle's waterfront, to be exact, in the Ye Olde Curiosity Shop. In his book *Alias Soapy Smith*, Jeff Smith, Soapy's great-grandson, makes a good case for Sylvester being one and the same mummy as McGinty. Smith has a photo of the figure Soapy called McGinty in the family collection (see page 44). The photo was taken after Soapy had vacated Creede and returned to life in Denver. The photograph, though overexposed likely due to a bright flash, shows a body in the exact same position as Sylvester's is today. McGinty appears to be roughly the same size as Sylvester as well.

The Sylvester mummy has been studied extensively, according to the Ye Olde Curiosity Shop's webpage. Here's what it has to say about his origins and the results of the tests that have been run:

Who is Sylvester? Legends abound. He was a cowpoke who got drunk, passed out in the Arizona sun, died there and was double-crossed by his guide and left for dead in the desert. He was John Wilkes Booth, Abraham

Lincoln's assassin. He was a Wild West desperado shot off his horse, stripped and discovered in a sand dune by two wandering riders in the Gila Desert of 1895. We don't know for sure…and he isn't talking.

In some ways, his afterlife is even more colorful. He was exhibited at Seattle's Alaska Yukon Exposition of 1909 and at San Francisco's Panama-Pacific Exposition of 1915. He's toured with sideshows and carnivals. He even ended up as a sofa—well, in a sofa—as the punchline to a practical joke. (The dentist who purchased him for $35 thought it would be great fun to slip him under a false bottom he built under the cushions of his sofa, then show his guests what they'd been sitting on.)

It's not that we haven't tried to learn about him. Subjected to the intense gaze of scientific inquiry, the mummy has been x-rayed and has endured several thousand MR and CT scans collected as recently as 2005. These have shown that all his internal organs, including his brain and delicate optic nerves, are present. Jerry Conlogue, a member of the examining team, was moved to say that Sylvester "is the best-preserved mummy we have studied." Might have something to do with the fact that the body is infused with arsenic, an antique yet effective preservative.

But there's just so far science can go. X-rays of his bones may show he probably didn't dig ditches for a living, but who is he? Who is Sylvester? What we know about Sylvester

* Age at death: 35–40 years old
* Current weight: 137 pounds
* Weight at death: 240 pounds, approximately
* Probably at least chubby, if not fat; "wet"-looking areas of body are exuded lipids (fats)
* Body preserved with arsenic, process in use since Civil War
* Skeleton indicates he was not a laborer
* Gunshot blast didn't kill him. Steel pellets did not penetrate scalp, though he was shot from fairly close range. They are completely healed over, probably several years before death. For some reason, he never sought medical attention.
* MRI and CT images collected November 19, 2005, show all internal organs preserved at two-thirds original size[29]

The amount of arsenic used in preserving this mummy was considerable, and scientists concluded that the body was not preserved for burial but for display. Preserved for display sometime post–Civil War, this man was not a laborer but perhaps earned his money as a professional gambler. He was shot at close range by a shotgun and survived but did not seek medical attention for his injuries. This could easily indicate that he was at that point on the run from the law or an enemy. All of these findings seem consistent with Jeff Smith's theory that this man could have in life been the Louisiana Kid.[30] In summing up his theory, Smith stated:

> *Over the decades I collected digital photographs of petrified bodies and mummies. Very, very few are even remotely close to looking similar to others. They all take on their own "personalities," body shapes, location of limbs, as the years pass. With that in mind, what are the mathematical odds that two intentionally petrified bodies that look near identical, end up in the same state, in the same year (1895) and BOTH with gunshot wounds! That last part is important as they are the ONLY two petrified men known to have bullet wounds!*

I lived in Seattle's Belltown neighborhood for many years just blocks from the waterfront and Ye Olde Curiosity Shop. Countless times I wandered through that shop, marveling at specimens like the two-headed snake floating in a jar of formaldehyde, an eight-legged pig, the absolutely chilling shrunken head collection, the creepy "mermaid," but most especially the mummies. These gruesome and ghastly curiosities are completely fascinating. Imagine my amazement to find out some years later that the Sylvester mummy could indeed have a connection to my tiny hometown in the mountains of southern Colorado. If you see this mummy, you will not mistake it for being cement or stone. You can observe every hair of Sylvester's mustache, look at each crooked, decaying tooth in his shriveled grimace, even gaze into the cloudy eyes themselves, which are disturbingly half-open. Observation of these details brings to mind the words from a handbill Soapy used to advertise McGinty: "A petrification as natural as life, showing a fine specimen of manhood; every muscle, and even pores of the skin are plainly seen by the naked eye."[31]

Another wanderer fascinated by the macabre collection at Seattle's Ye Olde Curiosity Shop had a spooky encounter with Sylvester and a female mummy dubbed Sylvia displayed alongside him. The man later wrote this eerie account on his blog:

> *Having never seen a "mummy" I initially found the exhibit rather anti-climactic. These mummies, and indeed most mummies, do not look authentic.*

Regardless of how "well-preserved" they are in an archaeological sense, they seem less like dead people, and more like the stain of human likeness after all remnants of bodily and spiritual life have been blasted beyond recognition. I remember, there, trying to search for the humanity in the pair. Perhaps, I could piece together what the mummies must have looked like in life, adding on hair, muscle, and flesh in my imagination and until the figures looked like recently deceased corpses. The effort proved to be futile, but as I lethargically ambled towards the exit, a visceral sensation seized my mind. I now find it hard to explain, but at that moment an image of the larger mummy, Sylvester, became immediately visible; not as a desiccated husk, or even as a recently deceased corpse, but as the man that he must have been once in life. And then it seemed as if there was an essence, as alive as any of the shop patrons, trapped within his dried and mangled form. An uneasy feeling took me as I exited the shop.

This vision persisted long into the evening that day, returning later as a nightmare. Though I only have a vague recollection of this, I remember that in the dream I had taken the place of Sylvester behind in the glass display, paralyzed, with a frozen gaze peering out across the shop. However, this time, something was very different. The image I saw before me was hardly the lively boutique I had experienced in my waking state. Instead, the patrons were frozen in place with glassy-eyed stares, and it was as if the entire outside world had been coated in a thick waxy pollution that robbed even the woodwork, earth, and outside sky of life. In the true nature of role reversals, just as my life had was now inside the mummy, the lifeless process of mummification had seized the rest of reality and drained it of its essence.

Even after this dream left me, my mind lingered on the fearful notion that what I had seen was prophetic and that this sort of living death in which all of reality is frozen in eternal lifelessness might be what waits for all sentient creatures at the moment of their demise.[32]

Truly a terrifying dream if you ask me. For one's consciousness to remain trapped within a dead and decaying (or even preserved) body is probably the worst fate imaginable. Was the flash this man saw of the mummy as he was in life exactly as the Louisiana Kid appeared that night as he "headed south on the pike" trying to escape the wild Creede Camp wounded and dying that cold February evening? If he could describe to us what the fleshed-out mummy looked like in his vision, perhaps we would know more about what the Kid looked like as well.

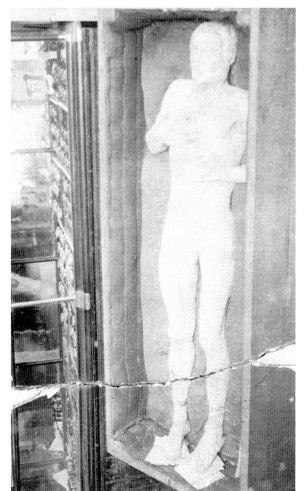 

Left: A photo of Soapy's petrified man, "McGinty," taken at one of his auction houses in Denver after leaving Creede. *Jeff Smith Collection*.

Right: The mummy "Sylvester" is still on display today along Seattle's waterfront at the Ye Olde Curiosity Shop. *Jeff Smith Collection*.

Should Jeff Smith's utterly bizarre and entirely plausible theory regarding the McGinty mummy and its creation from the human remains of the Louisiana Kid hold true, I'd venture to say there never was a soul more entitled to haunt Creede than that of the Louisiana Kid. Many cultures believe that the soul of an unburied person is unable to cross over to the afterlife and is cursed to wander the earth until the body is at last buried. And as for the current residents of Creede who have seen this zombie-like creature "searching for a bag at the water's edge," what makes them believe McGinty is searching for a bag? I would think it far more likely that he is searching for his body, never interred and still on display to the public as a morbid curiosity in a glass cabinet over one thousand miles away in Seattle.

3

BOB FORD'S DEATH IN CREEDE

The fundamental difference between the mystery story and the ghost story
is the fact that a mystery demands a solution for its effectiveness;
a ghost story is necessarily unsolvable.
—Bennett Cerf

L et's get this out of the way right up front; the ghost of this town's most infamous resident and outlaw does not haunt Creede. Just as the body of Bob Ford does not lie in the boot hill grave where he was initially buried, his spirit does not seem to have stuck around. I've never heard a story about Bob's ghost appearing in Creede, although I have searched, asked around and kept my fingers crossed that this ghost might make an appearance. If he does haunt Creede, he does so silently and without fanfare—in other words, completely in opposition to the way he lived in Creede. In life, the thirty-year-old Ford ran a boisterous gambling den and dance hall on the main street, complete with several sporting women. He dealt faro and officiated boxing matches alongside the famous Bat Masterson.

One April evening in 1892, he went on a drunken spree with his pal Joe Palmer, manager of Soapy Smith's Orleans Club. The two terrorized and shot up the town for hours, not stopping until they ran out of liquor and bullets. The *Creede Candle* reported that they "got on a raid and shot Jimtown full of holes. Buildings were perforated, window panes broken and the air badly cracked up with pistol balls."[33] Indiscriminately, they

Famous lawman Bat Masterson was a resident of Creede at the height of the boom. Though he was never officially a lawman here, some think his presence may have kept some semblance of order in the rowdy camp. *N.H. Rose Collection. Courtesy Western History Collections, University of Oklahoma Libraries.*

shot out streetlights and shop windows, terrorizing any poor soul who by necessity ventured out into the street by shooting at or near them until they flew for cover. In short, if Bob Ford's spirit were still in Creede, somebody probably would have noticed.

That nighttime mayhem with Joe Palmer resulted in both Bob and Joe hightailing it out of town rather than face a possible lynching. Bob was gone not much more than a week before his friends, including Jack Pugh, whom we will hear more of later, were able to smooth the feathers of angry townsfolk and make way for his return to Creede.[34]

Little more than a month after his return though, Bob Ford would be dead. He was brutally murdered in Creede almost exactly ten years after he killed one of the most notorious desperados of all time, Jesse James. Bob was caught unawares and gunned down in his own makeshift tent saloon on June 8, 1892, at close range by a sawed-off double-barreled shotgun in the hands of Ed O'Kelley.[35] This close-range load of buckshot struck him squarely in the neck, nearly decapitating him, and it is said that his opal and gold collar pin was driven into a tent post behind where he last stood. Legend has it this collar pin was later pried out and gifted to Soapy Smith as a good luck charm.[36] The circumstances of Bob Ford's death would seem the perfect scenario for creating an angry or confused spirit, yet nothing. Ford was buried on the mesa in Creede's boot hill cemetery on June 11, 1892. His body was exhumed later that same summer, and his wife, Dot Ford, accompanied his body back to Missouri, where he was buried near his brother Charley. Regarding the relocation, Edwin Bennett wrote: "After which she [Dot Ford] returned to Creede to go to work in Dave Sponsilier's dance hall. About that last, one old-timer was heard to remark, 'Guess she didn't want Bob's ghost watching her activities down at Dave's.'" Well, at least we have one plausible explanation why Bob Ford's ghost does not haunt Creede.

Left: Bob Ford shows off the pistol he used to kill Jesse James, circa 1883. *Courtesy of St. Joseph Museums Inc.*

Right: An older Bob Ford not long before he arrived in Creede, circa 1889. *Public domain.*

Locals gather for a photo as Bob Ford's body is removed from his tent saloon, June 1892. *John Gary Brown Collection.*

Left: Ed O'Kelley shot and killed Bob Ford in Creede on June 8, 1892. *N.H. Rose Collection. Courtesy Western History Collections, University of Oklahoma Libraries.*

Right: Robert Newton Ford. *N.H. Rose Collection. Courtesy Western History Collections, University of Oklahoma Libraries.*

In the absence of his spirit though, there are several unsolved mysteries regarding his death in Creede. I've always wondered where exactly his saloons were, first the two-story exchange that burned down in the fire of June 5, 1892, and the second, the tent saloon where he was shot and killed. What were the names of these saloons? What happened to the old wooden bar that was in the tent saloon at the time of Bob's death? How was it that in mid-February 1892 (nearly four months before the actual event occurred) a Colorado newspaper published a report that Bob Ford had been shot down and killed at the Creede Camp by Ed O'Kelley? For the answers to these questions, I turned to the historic newspapers and to accounts of several who claimed to be in Creede and even in the tent saloon at the time of the bloody assassination. As a consolation, I did eventually uncover one related ghost, though not Bob's—more on that later.

Poker Alice Tubbs was one of the most famous female gamblers of the West, and she worked for Ford in his Creede Exchange dealing faro. Here are some of her thoughts on Bob Ford himself and her firsthand account of his death:

It fell to my fortune to become a faro dealer in Bob Ford's place when at last, some time following the killing of Jesse James, he came to Creede.... Bob Ford I found to be an unobtrusive, commonplace persona of the down-Missouri type, and with none of the heralded mock bravado which he is said to have assumed after the killing of the Missouri bandit leader. More than that, to me at least, he denied that he was the slayer he was charged with being.

I often talked to him about Jesse's death. Why, I do not know, unless it was that Bob Ford seemed as anxious to confide in someone as I was anxious to have him talk. His plaint was always that he did not fire the shot which killed Jesse James, and that it was not even his plot thus to remove the bandit leader.

"It was Charlie's idea," he would tell me. Charlie was his brother, who, sometime following the murder, committed suicide. "As for myself, I was always afraid of Jesse. I was afraid of him when he and his gang used to come to our house in Missouri; and if I ever had aimed a gun at him, I would have trembled so I could not have hit him. But Charlie was different, and he is the one who fired the shot. Of course, I was in on the killing—I was there, and I knew that it was going to happen. But Charlie is the one who did the actual shooting—I didn't have the courage."

Perhaps if Bob Ford had taken a few other persons into his confidence he might not have been killed by Kelly, or O'Kelly—the slayer was known by both names—as he crossed his gambling hall that afternoon in Creede.

Bob Ford, if he had not been known as the slayer of Jesse James would not have created the slightest ripple in the West. He was of the inconspicuous type, neither prepossessing nor over-powering in appearance; he would have been merely one of the crowd. But the notoriety of his alleged deed made him stand forth, and made others wish to stand forth upon what they believed would be a pedestal erected to the avenger of a bandit about whom tradition and controversy had built up a sort of halo. Jesse James was as much of a hero to many as he was a vicious character to others. I know at least one man who celebrated himself into a terrific headache when Bob Ford was killed.

Kelly wanted notoriety. A cub reporter came to Creede to write up the town. One of the persons he met was Kelly, and one of the things Kelly told him was that he intended to kill Bob Ford. The reporter, being a faithful soul, sent in the prediction and it was printed. There was nothing for Kelly to do then but to make good on his promise and do it quickly—before Bob Ford could read the paper.

Famous lady gambler "Poker Alice" Tubbs lived in Creede during its boom and reminisced about those days in her later years. *N.H. Rose Collection. Courtesy Western History Collections, University of Oklahoma Libraries.*

I had just gone off shift and was standing near the bar. Bob Ford was there also, drinking. From the rear of the establishment, Ford's wife summoned him and he turned to answer, halting in the middle of the dance floor as someone shouted his name from the doorway. He half turned to see who was there. A terrific report sounded from a shotgun and Bob Ford dropped to the floor with his head almost torn from his neck by a charge of buckshot fired by the killer Kelly. I had often wondered whether it would have happened if Bob Ford had announced publicly what he told me in private. Perhaps Kelly would not have felt so much pride in shooting a man who had confessed to being afraid to pull a trigger.[37]

Alice's account certainly does shed a different light on the character of Bob Ford. She seems to believe Ford's claim that he did not actually fire the bullet that killed Jesse James. The portrait she paints of Bob Ford's character is quieter and less assuming than that drawn by most. Far from a braggart proud of slaying the outlaw Jesse James, Bob denied the deed and even seemed contrite about the part he played in the drama. Alice's account also seems to solve the mystery of the seemingly psychic newspaper prediction that Ford would be killed by O'Kelley in Creede. O'Kelley was simply making good on what he had promised the reporter he would do. However, it took nearly four months for his hatred to fester and to find the right opportunity to get this job done, and Ford had certainly read the article. Bob Ford reportedly laughed off that prediction, calling it "the veriest kind of a canard," or unfounded rumor.[38] There's no doubt that Bob's already anxious nature became more heightened after that.

In an interview published in *Colorado Magazine* in 1944, San Luis Valley rancher and one-time boomtown Creede livery operator William A. Braiden told this story regarding Bob Ford's death:

> *Living in Creede at that time was certainly not dull. One evening, I was eating in a small restaurant across the street from Bob Ford's saloon; my table companion seemed to have spent much of the afternoon in his cups, and was having considerable difficulty in maintaining a sitting position while he guzzled a bowl of oatmeal. Zing! A stray bullet from the saloon sang through the window, hit the bowl of oatmeal squarely and scattered it all over the table. My drunken friend set up an outcry for another bowl of mush; I do not know who served him, for the waiter and I had made a hasty exit by way of the back door.*
>
> *On June 5, 1892, fire practically destroyed the business section of Creede. Both Bob Ford and I were burned out. We moved down on the school section and each of us rebuilt his business, about two hundred feet apart. One morning as my foreman and I were saddling up the horses, we heard a shot; he immediately dashed into the saloon. I proceeded more cautiously; as I started into the building, I ran spank into Bob Kelley [sic], who was walking out of the saloon, gun in his hand, and a grin on his face. I hurried through the door; what a sight met my eyes! There lay Bob Ford on the floor, a bullet had cut his throat; blood covered the place; his wife was kneeling over him sobbing. I had enough and left hurriedly. We buried Bob, next day, up on the hill. I furnished the hearse, a Concord spring wagon, and my brother, Sam, acted as driver; later the body was removed and sent back to Missouri. Bob Ford would no more boast of killing Jesse James![39]*

Braiden mentioned that both his livery and Ford's gambling hall were burned out in the big fire of June 5, 1892, and then moved to the school section of town. Where was Ford's gambling hall that burned down? According to a map of the burnt district in Leland Feitz's *Quick History of Creede*, "Bob Ford's House" stood just north of the present-day location of the Mineral County Courthouse. Often this business is referred to by the papers as Bob Ford's Creede Exchange. An old photo from John Gary Brown's collection has a handwritten notation over a storefront in the location where Ford's saloon is supposed to have been. On the storefront, someone has written two unintelligible words and "Bob Ford." I'm almost certain that the labeled business is indeed Ford's two-story gambling parlor and dance hall. We may not know the exact name, but we now know what his exchange looked like.

As for the tent saloon's location, research shows that the school section of town to which Braiden referred was most of the land south of Wall Street. Another clue about the location is an old boulder that now sits on the west side of Main Street just south of Second Street in a grassy area next to the Wild Beaver Emporium. This land would indeed be in what was considered the school section. The boulder has been there for as long as I can remember, and I've yet to find anyone who knows when it was placed there or who installed the plaque on it that reads: "Creede,

Kinneavy's Sample Room sits at the junction of Cliff Street and Creede Avenue (Main) in Jimtown. This is where the June 5, 1892 fire began. On a business front, to the right is a handwritten notation indicating "Bob Ford," most likely Ford's Creede Exchange. *John Gary Brown Collection.*

Colorado, This is the approximate site of Bob Ford's saloon. Ford, the slayer of Jesse James was killed here on June 8, 1892 by Ed O'Kelly." I remember being fascinated by this as a child but also being told that the plaque was likely inaccurate. In fact, most people in Creede, if they've even noticed the boulder with its claim of being the location of Ford's tent saloon, will tell you it is not correct. When creating a route for my ghost tour, I even left this potential stop off because I was so convinced of its falsehood. One afternoon, as I was sifting through an internet collection of photos of Bob Ford's death, I came across a picture that nearly took my breath away. It is a photo of Ford's tent saloon that I had never seen before, and it is numbered by the photographer as 108 in a series. Photograph 109 from that same series is the most often seen and published photo of Bob Ford's death and is a close-up shot of the tent saloon surrounded by people parting as a wagon approaches to remove the body (see page 48). It is aptly titled *Death of 'Bob' Ford, removing the body, 109.* The new picture is titled *108 The place of 'Bob' Ford's death June 8th, 1892* and is taken from farther south and at a wider angle. Behind the tent saloon and other storefronts, you can clearly see the mountains and cliffs that are so unique to Creede's landscape. The moment I saw this photo, I knew that the boulder and plaque were in the correct location. To confirm my theory, I immediately called on my friend David Clark, author of *Bob Ford, Jesse James' Killer Shot Down in Creede.* David and I have had several discussions about the whereabouts of that tent saloon, and I asked him to go to the spot and attempt to re-create the new photo I was about to send him. The results were "pretty darn convincing," as David would later say. The location of that boulder is nearly spot on when the mountains and cliffs are lined up with those in the old photo (see page 55). For me, this was an exciting revelation and another of history's mysteries was solved. Apparently, I'd had the answer all along and just did not trust that the stone was correct.

I solved another mystery for myself upon reading *Creede Chronicle* editor and poet Cy Warman's firsthand account of June 8, 1892, in a story he wrote called "A Quiet Day in Creede." In his account, he calls Bob Ford's tent saloon the "Leadville dance hall" and tells of the day's events leading up to and including Ford's murder:

> *The report of the shotgun startled the whole camp, and as the Leadville was directly opposite my hotel, I rushed over and was almost the first man in the place. One man had preceded me, and as I entered he came out and shouted: "Bob Ford's dead."*

At the moment I entered the only person in the room was the insignificant looking woman in the little office. She was weeping. She knew me as the editor of the morning paper, and at once began to pour out the story of Bob's virtues. "He had planned," she said, "to do much good."

"....But say," she continued, waving a hand in the direction of the corpse, and her eyes filling with a fresh flood of tears, "just to think they should shoot him with that kind of a gun—it—just breaks my heart," and she leaned her head upon the bar and wept bitterly.

"Why Bob wouldn't uv killed a coyote with a shotgun. It's a coward's gun. When he killed Jesse James, the braves' man 'at ever lived an' the deadest shot, he dun it with a 45."

"Well," said I, glancing toward the rear of the room to make sure he was still there, "Bob's all right. He's a good fellow—now."[40]

It is clear that Ed O'Kelley chose a gun that would not allow him to miss, for if he did miss, he'd never get a second shot at Bob Ford. O'Kelley surprised Bob and murdered him in a brutal and unheroic way with a gun that others would not use to kill a coyote. But if he thought he'd be put on a

The boulder in the lower right corner marks the approximate location of Bob Ford's tent saloon, where he was murdered by Ed O'Kelley. *Photograph by David Clark.*

pedestal for ridding the world of Bob Ford, he was wrong. This killing was met with much the same reaction from the public as Bob Ford had received for shooting Jesse James in the back. O'Kelley was convicted of the murder and sentenced to life in prison.

From Cy Warman's account, we now know that the tent saloon was called the Leadville dance hall, but what ever became of the wooden bar that was in the saloon at the time of Ford's death? Warman's account claims that the wooden bar stretched down the right side of the tent with a small fence that extended from the end of the bar to the front of the tent, creating a small office. The dance floor was to the left. A photograph taken in June 1896 has the following text written across the bottom: "Bob Ford's (slayer of Jesse James) old bar, at which he was killed, Creede, Colo." In the picture, we see a dilapidated old white wall tent with a wooden bar standing outside of it. If the "old bar" refers to the actual piece of furniture and not the tent itself, we have a reference for what the bar might look like. The picture itself was taken far above Creede, up West Willow at the small townsite of Weaver.

The Creede Elks Lodge claims that the bar in its back lounge is the very one Ford was shot over, and the Elks have a weathered and crumbling

An 1896 photo of Bob Ford's "old bar," perhaps referring to the wooden bar sitting in front of the tent. *John Gary Brown Collection.*

handwritten letter stating this fact. The letter, written sometime around 1937, is framed and hangs near the bar. The letter reads:

Notice: This is the Bar at which Bob Ford was killed. It was in use in his tent Saloon in the city of Creede at that time. He was leaning over it, in conversation with his bartender at the time the fatal shot was fired. The tragedy occurred Sep. 2nd 1902, 35 years ago. His body was buried here but later Exhumed and taken to the family cemetery in Missouri. He was killed with a load of Buckshot fired from a gun in the hands of "Red" Kelly. Bob Ford was the murderer of the bandit Jesse James, it is presumed that Jesse's brother, Frank, hired Kelly to kill him.

There are some inaccuracies in the letter, including the date Ford was killed, but still, it could be valid. Examination of the Elks bar shows it to be more ornate than the bar in the photo taken at Weaver.

Another account found in a 1909 *Creede Candle* article describes an old pine bar found in one of the cabins at Spar City and claims that this is the bar that was once in Ford's tent saloon:

A Creede old timer came to Spar, and his story gave the bar a lustrious [sic] fame. "Why, that's the bar," he declared, "behind which Bob Ford, the fellow who killed Jesse James, was killed. It was sold to a Spar saloonkeeper and moved up here. Ford was shot in the back, just as he killed Jesse James."[41]

Spar City, which became a ghost town in the early 1900s, was then purchased in 1905 by a group of Kansas prohibitionists who turned the small mining town into a private summer retreat. The old pine bar that the Creede Candle claims was Bob Ford's is in a privately owned cabin and has yet to be compared to the photograph of the bar taken in Weaver. Perhaps the actual bar is sitting in the Elks Lodge lounge, or maybe it is in a cabin up at Spar City. Although there are several clues, the mystery of what happened to Bob Ford's old bar remains unsolved.

I did promise you, dear reader, a ghost story. The tale I know is that of a dark, maudlin lady shedding her tears on Creede's Main Street in the late hours of the evening and wee hours of the morning. This specter is Creede's own version of the famous La Llorona, the weeping woman. She is often heard and not seen. Those who have caught a glimpse of this ghost describe a tiny woman clad in a long black Victorian dress, hat and

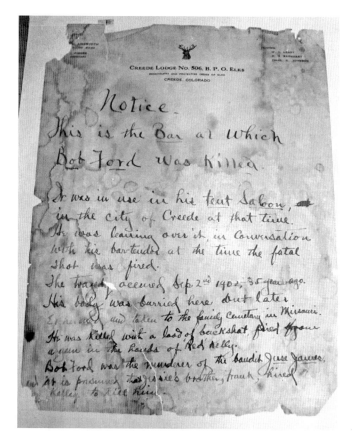

This notice hangs near the bar at the Creede Elks Lodge, BPOE No. 506. *Author collection.*

Three women are among those photographed during the removal of Ford's body. Could one of these be Dot Ford? *John Gary Brown Collection.*

veil. The veil obscures an alabaster face, and her weeping figure wanders aimlessly along Main Street. Her sobbing can be heard from far off, but the apparition vanishes if approached. Her heart-wrenching wails are said to bring tears to the eyes of anyone who hears them. I suspect that this desperate figure is the ghost of Bob Ford's widow, Dot. After his death, Dot Ford traveled to Lake City to await the trial of Ed O'Kelley. In an article announcing the guilty verdict, the *Salida Mail* described Dot in this way: "Mrs. Dot Ford has been at Lake City the past two weeks awaiting the trial. She is a small, slim lady, is dressed in deep mourning and has a sad and pale face denoting that she has passed through much trouble."[42] After the trial and her sorrowful journey to return Ford's body to his family plot in Missouri, a forlorn Dot did come back to Creede to earn her living by dancing at the Grand Theater. She was said to show off a bullet scar or powder burn on her arm, damage incurred in one of Bob's rampages. Dot Ford eventually remarried and moved to Durango, where she would commit suicide by overdosing on morphine in 1902.[43] Perhaps the Widow Ford's lost and troubled soul still searches in vain for Bob's along the streets of Creede where they last walked arm in arm.

4

THE BADDEST MAN IN CAMP

The muses are ghosts, and sometimes they come uninvited.
—Stephen King

It is the fall of 1997, and I am climbing the rickety stairs of an old Victorian home in Mancos, Colorado. The home is a renovation project in the works, and the bedroom where I will be sleeping nestles at the top of a narrow staircase. I'm not thinking about ghosts. In fact, ghosts are probably the furthest thing from my mind. I am the tour manager for the Creede Repertory Theatre's Young Audience Program and have been on the road with three actors, a minivan and a small set for nearly two months. We have performed all across the Four Corners area and stayed in one hotel after another. But tonight, our small company is being hosted by members of the Mancos Arts Council in their home. I'm thinking how nice it will be to sleep somewhere other than a hotel. I enter the small bedroom with its sloping, dormered ceiling, antique four-poster bed and patchwork quilt and quickly settle in to read before falling to sleep. It is not long before my eyelids grow heavy, and I turn out the light, immediately dropping off.

I dream that I am floating above a bed looking down at a small room in which two women fuss around a bed where a disheveled man lies groaning. They attempt to comfort him, adjusting pillows, cradling his hands. It is to no avail. The man is bleary-eyed, feverish, mumbling. Grimy long underwear covers his tall, thin frame, and I can see that in addition to the dirt, there are bloodstains near his stomach. The details are shockingly visceral, more realistic than any dream I have ever had. There is a faint smell of blood mingled with perspiration, the stench of decline. As I observe from my omniscient perspective, one of the women turns to the other, takes her by the shoulders and screams. Her earsplitting shriek jerks me from my dreamworld back into the room at the top of the stairs. In the way of dreams, I understand that the shriek signifies the man in the bed has died, and as my eyes fly open, I realize that I'm lying in the very bed that I was just observing in my dream. I sit bolt upright in the pitch blackness of the room. Adrenaline pumps through my veins as I scramble out of the bed. Completely disoriented, I feel my way around the walls of the room searching in terror for the light switch. It is the longest twenty seconds of my entire life. Once the light is finally on, I dress and sit in the rocking chair in the corner of the room, as far from the bed as I can get. For nearly two and a half hours, I sit waiting for the rest of the house to awake.

Still shaky, I hurriedly tell my friend and fellow CRT company member Becky about this nightmare before sitting down to breakfast. She thinks I should also tell our hosts; I do not. As we eat breakfast, Becky decides to tell the couple the tale herself. When she finishes, the woman turns to me with wide eyes and says, "Kandra, we just bought that bed at an antique auction. You are the first person to have slept in it!"

It wouldn't be until twenty years later, as I read old newspaper articles in search of tales for my ghost tour, that I would find the connection between that dream and my hometown of Creede. Let me tell you the story of Handsome Jack Pugh, Lillie Shields and William Rumidge.

Truly the stuff that Wild West lore is based on, Jack Pugh appeared in the Creede Camp early in 1891, if not before, and had long since earned the reputation of a "bad man."[44] Originally from Ohio, he arrived in Colorado in the 1870s and served as a marshal and deputy sheriff in several towns in nearby Gunnison County.[45] Being a man of the law, however, did not mean that Jack stayed out of trouble. He was first cross-wise with the law for assault in 1881.[46] In Monarch, in 1884, Jack got into a drunken fight over a hand of cards and pursued another man down the street with his knife, a pool cue and guns a blazing.[47] When he was arrested, he tore the warrant from the deputy's hands, ripped it up and went home to bed. The next day, two more men came to arrest Jack. They pulled him from bed and pistol whipped him. A doctor later reported that Jack had several head lacerations ranging from one-half to four inches in length.[48] The court found that the arresting deputy's actions were warranted.[49] Then, in 1887 in the town of Villa Grove, "Griff Williams pulled a shot gun on Jack Pugh here Monday night, but the latter jumped and caught it in time to direct the charge through the sidewalk."[50] Jack seemed adept at cheating death, but the Grim Reaper would eventually catch up with him one shadowy night between two steep canyon walls in Upper Creede.

Before the Creede Camp had a paper, Del Norte's *San Juan Prospector* ran a weekly column called "From Creede Camp." It is here where we first read in May 1891 that Jack Pugh had a stable and boardinghouse at "Willow Junction," right at the forks of Willow Creek, which is now referred to as "the Y."[51] In July 1891, he again appeared in the column: "Handsome Jack Pugh is building a neat little cottage."[52] Jack was appointed as the first deputy to serve the riotous and booming Creede Camp, receiving his commission from Saguache County.[53] Mineral County would not be formed until March 1893, and in its beginning the Creede Camp spanned the corners of three existing counties—Saguache, Hinsdale and Rio Grande.

> *Creede, the original location, lies in a narrow gulch on East Willow Creek, in the corner of Saguache County; "New Town," Gin Town, Jimtown, Creedmoor or Amethyst, yet without a settled name, is one mile down the creek into Hinsdale County and Wason is…situated in the valley and Rio Grande County.*[54]

Handsome Jack was reputed to be a great fellow when not drinking, but hell-on-wheels if he was.[55] A friend of the infamous Bob Ford, Jack was said to be one of the people who pulled strings to help Bob return to Creede after being kicked out of town in April 1892.[56] Not surprisingly, Jack played a principal role in Creede's very first gun fray when on Thursday evening, October 29, 1891, he and his pal Jack Fullerton shot up Willow Junction's McLeod Saloon, run by Jack Farris.[57]

> *In order that the excitement should be kept at a fever-heat, sleepers in the neighborhood of Farris's saloon were awakened during the small hours by a regular fusillade of small arms—some reporting as many as two or three hundred shots. Next morning, there were several shot holes through the saloon building—one through the transom and another through the side of the building….Jack Pugh was said to be the operator and outside of two or three ineffectual shots at Jack Farris, no one seemed to know what he was shooting at, as he didn't hit anything in particular.*[58]

A man stands amid the clamor on Creede Avenue at the height of the boom, circa 1891 or early 1892. *John Gary Brown Collection.*

This was the Wild West, and there were no consequences for this madcap shooting spree. The very next night, Jack made a "gun-play" on a man near Jimtown. Saturday night found him drinking and carousing at Charley Gregory's saloon, where he shot one man through the ankle and pistol whipped a second. The injured parties were described as innocent bystanders who may have stood up against Pugh in an argument he had with a third man.[59] On that Sunday afternoon, Jack Pugh and Jack Fullerton were taking an afternoon stroll "with their best girls."[60] As they passed over the bridge near the junction, shots were fired at them from inside a local woman's cabin.[61] Fullerton took a shot in the shoulder, and Jack Pugh was shot through his coat but received not a single scratch. It was later discovered that the shots were fired by barkeep Jack Farris, seeking revenge for his saloon being torn up by gunfire the previous Thursday. Fullerton's shoulder wound was considered fatal, and he was reported to be on his death bed.[62] The doctor in charge of Fullerton, however, successfully amputated the wounded arm at the shoulder, and Fullerton made a full recovery.[63] In 1893, "One-Armed Jack" Fullerton was in the Saguache jail for shooting at dance hall girl, Lillie Russell, while she was performing onstage in Creede at the Grand Theatre.[64] Jack Pugh, on the other hand, had escaped one more shoot-out unfettered by bullet or the law. With his luck about to run out, Jack's days in Creede were now numbered. The "Week at Creede" column closed out with these words:

> *The habitual drunkard is here in force and he manages to the great annoyance of decent people to keep beastly full day and night. It is almost impossible to get a good night's rest anywhere in town on the account of the howls of the maudlin set. Add to this disgraceful annoyance the terrorizing effects of the oft-repeated gun plays, and we have a condition of society that is exceedingly repulsive to every principle of good citizenship. A killing is looked for at any moment and but for bad marksmanship there would have been three or four bodies ready for burial.*[65]

It's easy to understand after reading these passages how unpredictable and chaotic life must have been in this boomtown and what likely inspired Cy Warman to pen his poem "There Is No Night in Creede."

Jack, also known as, J.L. Pugh, was not just a gunslinging drunkard—he was a successful businessman who owned the Creede Livery Feed and Sale Stable. Next to his house in Jimtown, that "neat little cottage" mentioned before, he had a wagon repair and tack barn, and across the way, on the

CREEDE LIVERY FEED & SALE STABLE.

J. L. PUGH, Proprietor.

Good Rigs and Saddle Horses.   Horses Boarded.

Jack Pugh's Creede Livery Feed & Sale Stable Advertisement, 1892. *From the* Creede Candle, *Colorado Historic Newspapers online..*

Thought to be the location of Jack Pugh's house, wagon repair and feed shop, and livery stable on the south side of the street. This picture was taken in 1893 after Jack's death, and the sign reads Creede Transportation Company. *Creede Historical Society Archives.*

south side of First Street, stood his sizeable livery stable.[66] In January 1892, the *Creede Candle* ran an article that described J.L. Pugh as "one of the first to get in and [he] has always taken a leading part in the progress of the camp. He is conducting a livery and feed business and investing in real estate and mines on the side."[67]

Jack's interest in real estate was not always lawful, as you can imagine, and lot or claim jumping was not limited to miners. In January 1892, Pugh spotted a lot in the center of the original Creede Camp that he felt would be perfect for the saloon he wished to build. When Mayor Osgood and his wife, the rightful owners of this lot, left town for a few days, Jack sprang into action. He "jumped the lot and had men working until midnight getting lumber with which to hold

Two men stand in the doorway of the Holy Moses Saloon in what is now North Creede. The man on the right is William Orthen, who would later become Lizzie Zang's second husband. *Denver Public Library, Western History Collection, X-7488.*

HOLY MOSES

SALOON,

J. G. OSGOOD, - - - - Proprietor

Holy Moses Saloon Advertisement, 1892. *From the* Creede Candle, *Colorado Historic Newspapers online.*

it."[68] Mrs. Osgood returned to Creede and immediately had Jack's lumber thrown from her lot. She then hired her own crew to begin building what would become the Holy Moses Saloon. Sources say she stood guard over the lot and the construction as her saloon went up board by board.[69] Pugh held a bitter grudge against the Osgoods, even though the lot was originally Mrs. Osgood's, and she was in the right.[70]

On May 4, 1892, Jack let his burning resentment lead him to the Holy Moses Saloon, where he began drinking early in the day.[71] Jack played poker, seven-up and whist with others while drinking heavily. Perhaps he was even dealt the dead man's hand of aces and eights. As the shadows of the cliffs closed in on the saloon and day faded to evening, he became more obnoxious. When City Marshal Pete Karg, another saloon keeper in Upper Creede, stopped by the Holy Moses around 5:00 p.m., Mayor Osgood, aware of Jack's animosity and vendetta, asked the marshal to stay and keep an eye on the matter. The mayor would later tell the *Creede Candle*:

> *About 10 o'clock Jack was* [more] *boisterous than ever. Somebody told Karg to arrest him. Karg told Jack that he was making too much noise, that he was drunk and ought to go home, talking to him quietly and arguing the case with him. At this Pugh got hot and wanted to fight. Then he caught hold of Karg and turned him around, saying that he could not arrest him and that he would kill him if he tried it. Karg called on some man to help him and broke loose from Jack and started to run to the rear of the saloon. As he did so Jack pulled his gun and started after him. Karg got his gun out and fired.*[72]

Jack Pugh was shot in the bowels by Karg's .44-caliber pistol and would remain semiconscious for several hours.[73] One paper reported:

> *As he fell Pugh exclaimed; "I am hurt," and later to Karg; "You have murdered me without reason," and to Osgood; "You have caused my death."*[74]

Lillie Shields, the woman who lived with Pugh, arrived at the Holy Moses Saloon and took him back home, which the paper reports was next to the sporting house of notorious gambler and madam Minnie Smith.[75] At the age of only thirty-eight, Jack passed away in his own bed early the next morning. One newspaper wrote, "At Creede, Jack Pugh, the original bad man of the camp, died with his boots on."[76] Dying with one's boots on implied a violent death, and it is that phrase that led to graveyards for the criminal element being dubbed "boot hills." Following his wishes, Pugh's body was buried later that week in Del Norte by his "best girl," Lillie Shields. Perhaps he did not wish to be sent to Creede's boot hill. Lillie was said to be the only one to accompany the body to the grave.[77]

Lillie, or Lil, Shields was sometimes described as Jack's mistress, sometimes his wife or "reputed wife" and sometimes just the woman with whom he lived. It seems likely that Lillie was Jack's mistress. She was never once named as Mrs. Jack Pugh, as was the custom of the day when writing about a married woman. In that period, married women rarely kept their own last names, and in every instance, the papers give her surname as Shields. How did Jack and Lillie meet? It is pure speculation of course, but there were only a handful of reasons a single woman might come to a boomtown like Creede. One of them was to work as a professional gambler, such as Poker Alice, but I think the circumstances of Lillie's next appearance in the paper might rule that out. It is not a huge stretch to imagine that Lillie came to the Creede Camp as a dance hall girl or prostitute. Jack did live next to Minnie Smith's "sporting house," after all.

Whatever the circumstances, Lillie stayed on in Jack's house after he passed away. It is possible that she even took it into her own hands to avenge his death. Someone certainly seems to have. Less than a week after Jack Pugh's death, at around 2:30 a.m. on Tuesday May 10, an unknown person attempted to set fire to the Holy Moses Saloon.[78] But for the vigilant eye of a citizen and the quick actions of "Night Watchman Therien," the entirety of North Creede might have gone up in flames that night. Under one corner of the saloon, they found "shavings of wood, etc., saturated with coal oil" and concluded that the "dastardly job was the work of incendiaries."[79] Although the paper reported that the police had several clues that would "likely lead to the arrest of the fire fiend," it was never mentioned in the papers again.[80] Perhaps this fire fiend was Lillie; perhaps it was another of Jack's friends seeking revenge. Maybe it was even Bob Ford, who had, in part due to Jack's help, been allowed by then to return to Creede after his banishment at the end of April. Interestingly, this attempted arson occurred less than a month before another more catastrophic fire obliterated most of Jimtown.

Whether she was the arsonist or not, Lillie seems to have picked up and moved on with her life. Not long after Jack's death she reconnected with a former lover, twenty-four-year-old William Rumidge.[81] She and "Billy" were living it up on the evening of May 24, drinking and gambling in the Junction Saloon, which sat at "the Y" in Upper Creede. As the evening progressed, Billy began to tease Lillie:

Rumidge would frequently make tantalizing remarks about women's playing, which exasperated her to such an extent that she drew her revolver and threatened to shoot. To this he remarked, "If you pull your little popper on me I shall have to use my gun," and threw his weapon on the table.

Mr. Davis, the proprietor, interfered and both weapons were put away. Rumidge then continued his joshing, when Lillie picked up her chips and threw them in his face. The proprietor again interfered and the game was stopped. All stepped up to the bar for a drink.[82]

If only it had ended there. But no, Billy just had to make one more comment. Lillie pulled her "little popper," and when Billy reached out to take it from her, the pressure from both their hands on her hammerless pistol caused it to discharge. Unbeknownst to anyone but him, Billy was shot just to the left of his navel. He then exited the back of the saloon. When he staggered in the front door moments later, he called out, "Go for the doctor."[83]

The proprietor said: "You ain't hurt are you, Bill?"

"Yes, she got me all right," was the answer, at the same time opening up his clothes and showing where the shot had entered.

Three men stand in the doorway of the Junction Saloon where East Willow and West Willow Creeks meet. This is where Lillie Shields would accidently and fatally shoot Billy Rumidge. *Creede Historical Society Archives.*

This exhibition unnerved the woman. She almost went into hysterics and between her sobs moaned, "Oh, Billy, I did not mean it."
"Well, let's go home," he said, and handed her the pistol.[84]

The doctor was summoned and gave the couple the heartbreaking news that the wound was "necessarily fatal." Lil did take Billy home, and "he was placed in the same bed occupied by Jack Pugh, suffering from a pistol wound three weeks ago."[85] She turned herself in to the authorities, only to be released to nurse the dying man until such time as she was no longer needed. Billy lingered until around noon the next day, when he took his last breath right there in Jack Pugh's bed—but not before absolving Lillie of any intent to kill.[86]

I realize now that long before I ever read this account in the newspaper archives, I had witnessed this death in my dream in an antique four-poster bed at the top of a tall staircase in an old Victorian home in Mancos, Colorado. Could Jack Pugh's bed have traveled from one owner to the next and made its way west to Mancos? Or were the ghosts of Creede simply reaching out to me even then to come back and tell their stories?

My friend Susan Madrid is the current owner and resident of what I believe to have been the exact location and possibly the actual "neat little cottage" built by Jack Pugh, and she had no ghost stories to report when

Aspen Daily Leader headline, May 25, 1892. *Colorado Historic Newspapers online.*

I first asked her about it a few years back. Since then, my summer Ghostly Walking tour has stopped in front of the house several times, and the nearly unbelievable story of Jack and Billy dying in the same bed from almost identical gunshot wounds in the span of only three weeks has been relayed to each group. Ghost or no ghost, these stories of Jack, Lil and Billy were just too extraordinary not to tell. At the end of that first summer, Susan pulled me aside and said, "I'm not sure if your stories have roused the ghosts or just awakened my imagination." Curiously, paranormal phenomenon were now occurring. Occasionally, Susan would hear phantom guitar melodies drifting

Jack Pugh's house as it appears today. *Author collection.*

through the rooms of her house, and although she searched, no source for these tunes was ever located—inside or out. In addition to this ghostly music, whispering voices and muffled conversations floated from empty rooms in the late hours of the night and wee hours of the morning.

By the time the second summer season of the Ghostly Walks had wrapped up, Susan had another tale to share—and the ghosts were getting bolder. Late one night, she was lying in bed surfing the web on her phone when the lights in her room suddenly clicked off. She could tell that the electricity in the rest of the house was still on because she could see a bit of light glowing from a small lamp left on in the living room beyond her bedroom door. Feeling unsettled, she started to get up. Before her feet could hit the floor, Susan felt and heard a banging from underneath the bed. Truly terrified at this point, she exclaimed, "Jack Pugh, you leave me alone!" The lights in her room instantly snapped back on, and she huddled under her covers wondering what in the heck had just happened.

A former member of the acting company at the Creede Repertory Theatre, upon hearing my unfortunate account of Jack, Lil and Billy, told me his own tale. One evening following a performance, he and his girlfriend had taken a late-night stroll up the canyon toward North Creede. "It really is the best place to go star-gazing, you know, once you're away from all the streetlights," he said. Enveloped in the velvety black night and enjoying each other's company, the couple strolled along hand in hand. Under the glittering band of the Milky Way, Willow Creek was running high and fast with melting snow, and the runoff rumbled over the rocks surging past them toward the Rio Grande. As they approached the bridge at the Y, my friend saw the shadowy figure of a pale man in a cowboy hat and vest clutching his stomach and shuffling along the railing toward them. Startled, he turned to his girlfriend and said, "What do you think that guy's doing out here so late?"

"What guy?" she asked.

"Don't you see him? Right there," he said pointing to the spot on the bridge. But the figure was gone. Perhaps he saw the ghost of Billy Rumidge, returned to the scene of his accidental and fatal shooting right in that very spot where the Junction Saloon once stood. If you are interested in ghost hunting, you might want to take an evening stroll up to North Creede, do some stargazing and perhaps encounter the ghost of Billy Rumidge for yourself. And should a loud banging wake you in the night, just tell Jack Pugh to leave you alone!

5

THE MANY SPIRITS OF THE ZANG (CREEDE HOTEL)

What is a ghost? A tragedy condemned to repeat itself time and time again? An instant of pain perhaps. Something dead which still seems to be alive. An emotion suspended in time like a blurred photograph, like an insect trapped in amber.
—*Guillermo del Toro*

HISTORY OF THE HOTEL

If you ask anyone in Creede today where the town's ghosts might be found, the first answer you are likely to hear is at the Creede Hotel. One of the few buildings to have survived since Creede's boom days, the old hotel has seen its fair share of tragedy, including several deaths, a rape allegation and an attempted suicide, not to mention the many nights of restless and interrupted sleep. It was built by John and Lizzie Zang in the early months of 1892 and was originally called the Zang Hotel.[87]

John and Lizzie were childhood sweethearts who grew up together in the small village of Hostenbach, Germany. They immigrated to the United States shortly after they were married in March 1880 and came to Colorado. The couple first ran a boardinghouse in Georgetown and then moved on to Denver, where they had a hotel near Thirty-Sixth and Market Streets.[88]

In the early part of 1892, as Creede's boom peaked, John and Lizzie, now in their thirties, followed the crush of people to Creede, where they built the Zang Hotel. This original hotel stood on nearly the same spot as it now stands, only it was grander.[89] They did a splendid business for a few months until the big fire swept through Jimtown on June 5, 1892, burning everything in its path to the ground. They lost nearly everything, but John Zang was able to rebuild "on his old location in the burned district," and the Zang Hotel was opened again before the end of July 1892.[90]

John and Lizzie ran the hotel for many years, occasionally leasing it out to others while they tried their hand at other ventures, such as during the summer of 1894, when they ran the Hot Springs Hotel (where the 4UR Ranch is now located).[91]

In an email correspondence with one of Lizzie's living relatives, a great-niece, she relayed an old family story once told by Lizzie regarding the one and only time the infamous Bob Ford, slayer of Jesse James, came into the Zang Hotel. Bob was cursing a blue streak, which offended Lizzie greatly, especially since there were children present at the time. She walked over and asked Ford to please refrain from such language or kindly leave her establishment. He ignored her, turned back to his companion and continued to curse, at which point, Lizzie slapped him hard, nearly knocking him from his chair. Bob quickly rose to his feet, got quite close

The decimated Jimtown business district after the fire of June 5, 1892. *John Gary Brown Collection.*

Zang's Hotel newly rebuilt after the fire in June 1892. Note the charred ground to the right and piles of burnt debris in the background. The hotel was reopened in late July 1892. *Creede Historical Society Archives.*

to Lizzie's face and hissed, "If you were a man, you would no longer be living." Then he turned tail and left.

The Zangs would, however, long outlast Bob Ford, who was murdered in his Creede saloon on June 8, 1892. And unlike Ford, they were well liked throughout the camp. The local newspaper often made mention of them, their famed hospitality and their love for fishing. It was once noted that Lizzie spent an entire week fishing on Crooked Creek.[92] One of John's fishing escapades was written up:

> *John Zang, the good-natured German who looks after the Zang Hotel, went out fishing one day last week, but perhaps we should not tell of him falling into the river. It would never have been mentioned had Mr. Zang brought us home a fine fry as he promised.*[93]

Lizzie's renowned skills as a hostess and cook were also noted. One blurb read:

> *Judging from the way a great many of our boys stay closely to Zang's Hotel, it is sure that the meals at that house are what they are advertised.*[94]

In March 1905, the Zangs celebrated their silver wedding anniversary with an elegant dinner party in the dining room of the hotel. The *Candle*

Four children sit atop a burro in front of the Zang Hotel Office and Annex, date unknown. *Creede Historical Society Archives.*

A woman strolls past Zang's Sample Room on Wall Street. This is where salesmen displayed their goods. *Denver Public Library, Western History Collection, X-7475.*

reported that the two were dressed as they were when they were first married, including Mrs. Zang's "original wedding trousseau" right down to the bouquets.[95] There was much gaiety, and "singing and dancing was indulged in until late in the evening." John and Lizzie were described as "jovial and good-hearted people," and one could tell there was genuine affection shining through the words of the *Candle*'s reporter.

Five years later, the paper ran an article describing another celebration at the hotel, a grand surprise party that Lizzie threw for John on the occasion of his fifty-fifth birthday in December 1910:

> *Just a few of the friends of the happy couple were invited, it being manifestly impossible to invite every one of them for the reason that the hotel simply would not have held them all.*
>
> *A very nice supper was served to the assembled guests along about 9:30 pm and several little talks of congratulation were made by the guests. Of course, everything was in good old German style, and merriment reigned supreme. After supper, the guests beguiled themselves with cards until the small hours of the morning.*
>
> *We, in common with the rest of Johnny's many friends, wish him many more birthdays.*[96]

Sadly, there were not many more birthdays to come for John Zang; his fifty-fifth was to be his last. A shocking tragedy occurred only six months after that party, and it must have stunned the entire Creede Camp. On the Sunday afternoon of June 11, 1911, in what the *Creede Candle* called "one of the most horrifying murders in the history of the Creede District," John Zang was shot in the head at very close range with a .45-caliber Colt revolver and instantly killed by a woman named Fannie Lefevre at her home in Stringtown.[97] John had visited the LeFevre home while Mr. LeFevre was away. According to Mrs. LeFevre, John Zang attacked and attempted to molest her. After a struggle, she was able to break from his grasp, run to the kitchen and grab the gun. Frantically, she ordered him to leave her home. Four times she repeated this request, and when he refused

Creede Candle headline, June 17, 1911. *Colorado Historic Newspapers online.*

Above: A view of Stringtown with the railroad tracks running along the west side, businesses and residences along the east wall of the canyon and Willow Creek running through the middle, date unknown. *John Gary Brown Collection.*

Left: Stringtown taken from above the water tower, date unknown. *John Gary Brown Collection.*

and struck her in the eye, she turned the gun on him, firing into his face. The *Creede Candle* reported:

> *Without expressing any opinion upon the case either one way or the other, we will say that Mr. Zang's side of the story will never be known. The evidence given by the self-confessed murderess was of sufficient strength to cause a jury to claim that the shot had been fired in self-defense and thus acquit the woman of premeditation.*[98]

When this news was broken to Lizzie, the paper reported:

> *Her grief became uncontrollable and she obtained possession of a revolver of rather ancient make and attempted to make away with herself. She was disarmed by friends, but her spirit seems to be utterly broken by the fearful calamity that has overtaken her.*[99]

A few days later, John's funeral was held at Creede's Roman Catholic church, the same church that now sits on the mesa above town. Lizzie would then travel by train to Denver with John's body, laying him to rest in Denver's Riverside Cemetery.[100]

Lizzie Zang was a strong woman, and she bounced back from this tragedy to keep her hotel operating. Eight years later, on Thanksgiving Day 1919, she married William Orthen, a "mining man" and another of the Creede Camp's longtime residents.[101] Over the years, Lizzie would hang on to the

Above: Zang's Hotel Advertisement, 1907. The American Plan indicates that meals were included in the price of lodging. *From the* Creede Candle, *Colorado Historic Newspapers online.*

Right: Three women converse outside the Creede Hotel, December 1942. *Library of Congress; photograph by Andreas Feininger.*

hotel, sometimes leasing it and sometimes running it herself. A few of her summers were spent running the Antler's Ranch, bringing her that much closer to the Rio Grande and allowing her to squeeze in a bit more time fishing.[102] According to her great-niece, Lizzie remained in Creede until her death from cancer at the age of nearly seventy-two. Her body is buried alongside her first husband, John Zang, in the Riverside Cemetery in Denver. The headstone reads "Elizabeth Orthen 1859–1931."

GHOSTLY ENCOUNTERS

The Creede Hotel ghost stories were the first I remember hearing as a child and thus the earliest tales in my collection. My aunt Jennie Kay Hosselkus worked at the hotel, and I remember many breakfasts in that old dining room. Jennie Kay would make her famous smiley-face pancakes and tell me of her latest ghostly encounters. Here are a few of my favorite tales from Jennie Kay and others associated with the Creede Hotel.

The Creede Hotel as it appeared in 1985. Note the broken balcony post on the left corner. *Jeff Smith Collection.*

Billboard advertisement on the south end of the balcony at the Creede Hotel, 1985. *Jeff Smith Collection.*

A Hair-Raising Experience

Jennie Kay worked at the hotel in the late 1970s and early 1980s. During those days, it was in rough shape, with crumbling stucco covering the building. It was painted a drab tan with a darker brown, badly chipped trim. One of the posts holding up the front balcony had been knocked out when a drunken patron backed his car into it at the close of a celebratory evening at the bar. The post was hastily repaired, but the balcony always seemed to list a bit after that. The interior was not much better, with peeling red brocade wallpaper and terribly scuffed woodwork, all contributing to a dreary and somewhat spooky atmosphere. Jennie Kay performed several jobs at the hotel, cooking breakfast in the mornings and then cleaning rooms. One afternoon, she climbed the stairs to clean and turn over what is now called the Calamity Jane room, first on the left, just off the balcony. As she worked, she began to feel as if she were being watched, like she was not alone. She became quite uneasy and hurried her cleaning along as her apprehension grew. Finally, she came to the last task, changing the bed. By now, her apprehension had turned to dread, and she told herself, "Just get these sheets changed and you can get out of here!" The terror she felt welling in her chest was real, but she had a job to do and she was bound and determined to finish it. As she hurriedly tugged and smoothed the sheets over the mattress, she happened to look up and across the bed, only to catch a glimpse of herself in the vanity mirror across the room. A scream of surprise and horror escaped her lips when she saw that every hair on her head was standing straight on end! Dropping the pillows, she bolted from the room and down the stairs to the street, vowing to never return to the second floor of the hotel again.

A Haunted Happening at the Hotel

Several years later, in the dead of winter, Jennie Kay and her husband Kurt had just returned to town from seeing a movie in Monte Vista. As it closed in on midnight, they drove into Creede. A heavy snow had started to fall, and as was their custom, they drove up Main Street, turned around in the courthouse parking lot and proceeded back down Main to their home on Wall Street. I think everyone in Creede does this when they roll back into town, day or night—we used to call it "dragging the gut." When they pulled into their driveway, Jennie Kay remarked, "I wonder what was going on at the hotel tonight?"

Kurt looked confused and said, "What are you talking about?"

"Well, there was some kind of party going on. Didn't you see the people in there playing cards?"

"No. It's the middle of winter. No one was in there!"

"Yes! I think it might have been a costume party."

Kurt, intrigued, started up the truck again and drove right back up Main Street and past the dark and unmistakably deserted Creede Hotel.

Jennie Kay said she still gets chills thinking about that night and how clearly she saw that boisterous party. She remembers distinct details like a bearded, laughing man in a vest holding a hand of cards and sitting at the table by the window and recalls the way the light spilled out onto the December snow through the lace curtains.

It is interesting to note that in paranormal circles, there is a phenomenon called a residual haunting. It is described as a recording of an energy or an imprint from a specific time. For the observer, it is like watching a filmstrip of a past event. Could Jennie Kay and Kurt have driven past the hotel on December 15, the anniversary of John Zang's birthday? Was the merrymaking Jennie Kay witnessed that snowy winter evening the surprise birthday party that Lizzie threw for her beloved husband in 1910? That birthday celebration seems to have been one of the couple's last happy occasions at the business they began and ran together for so many years. Possibly the energy from that party has left its imprint on the hotel and replays itself once a year for those sensitive souls among the living who have the gift of seeing it.

The Old Lady with White Hair

In the mid-1980s, Rich and Cathy Ormsby decided to purchase the historic Creede Hotel. The hotel was nearly one hundred years old and had fallen into a state of disrepair. For their earnest money, they agreed to put a new roof on the now dilapidated old building. The Ormsbys were then living in a cabin in North Creede, the site of the original Creede Camp. Their home was about a mile and a half north of the hotel, and they walked into town one morning to work on the roof. In the late afternoon, dark clouds rolled in, bringing a heavy rainstorm, and they did not want to make the muddy trek back to North Creede in the downpour. At that time, the hotel had no heat or electricity, and they didn't even have a key, but Rich and Cathy found the kitchen door open. They determined to brave the night in one of the upstairs rooms. The room at the top of the stairs on the back side of the hotel, now called the Soapy Smith room, beckoned. So, as the rain continued to pour outside, they found a flashlight and some bedding and settled in for the night.

Several times during the night, Cathy reports that Rich would sit up in bed, shake his head and then drop back down on his pillow and return to sleep. She finally asked him what was wrong, and he muttered, "Oh, nothing. I must be dreaming; there can't be anything there." The next morning, she asked again what he had seen. He explained that he had repeatedly seen a woman standing in the doorway to their room. She was dressed in a long gown and had white hair that was pulled into a bun. He said she had been standing in the doorway, and although he couldn't see them, he felt that there were several other people in a line behind her, down the narrow stairwell. He told Cathy he believed these people had come to check in on them, to make sure they were okay.

A few years later, when Rich and Cathy were doing some remodeling on their new home behind the hotel, they again stayed in one of the rooms at the top of the stairs. This time, they slept in what is now the Poker Alice room, the second room down the hall on the back side of the hotel. One evening, Rich again dreamed of the old lady in her long gown. In this dream, he understood that she wanted to show him something. Gesturing for him to follow her, she drifted through the wall. The next morning, Rich told Cathy that he had really wanted to find out where the old woman might lead him. He had tried desperately to follow her but just could not get his body through the wall.

Several years passed, and the hotel, with its newly renovated rooms, fresh coat of paint, and unsurpassed homemade meals, had become a thriving business for the Ormsbys. All their hard work was paying off, and they hadn't thought of the old woman from Rich's dreams in a long time. While serving breakfast to her guests one morning, Cathy was asked by a well-dressed woman if they had any ghosts in the hotel. Cathy shrugged, replying that the hotel is an old building, and it was certainly possible. The woman then said, "Well, my husband has a story for you!" The couple had slept the previous night in the Poker Alice room, and the husband reported that he had been roused from sleep by a rustling sound. When he sat up to look around, he saw an old woman rifling through his wife's suitcase. She wore her hair in a bun and had on a long dress. Cathy recalled being startled that the description was a near perfect match for the old woman who had visited Rich in his dreams. The guest told the old woman, "Hey, those are my wife's things!" She ignored him and continued to sift through the suitcase, finally pulling out a pair of earrings and walking over to the vanity. She held the earrings up to her ears admiringly. When the husband again began to protest, the old woman gave him a look of defiance and simply vanished through the mirror. The next morning, the man wrote off this encounter as a bizarre dream, not thinking much of it until his wife, as she was dressing, asked, "Have you seen my earrings? I can't find them." He immediately walked over to the vanity to look. One of the earrings glinted in the morning sunlight on the floor nearby. The second earring was never found.

The Desk Clerk's Story, or Strange Bedfellows

One summer afternoon a few years back, I strolled past the hotel and decided to stop in and inquire about any recent ghostly activity. The desk clerk on duty confirmed that several guests report paranormal activity, often writing of their experiences in the journals kept in each room. He shared his favorite:

One evening, a couple rented a room at the hotel, and before retiring for the evening, they enjoyed a lovely dinner. They then climbed the winding stairs to their room, the Bat Masterson room, second on the left on the balcony side. The man stepped out on the balcony to read his book, while his wife went inside to shower and prepare for bed. Sometime later, the man began to feel drowsy. His eyelids heavy, he snapped his book shut and wandered into the room, donned his pajamas and crawled into bed next to his already sleeping wife. But as soon as he was in bed, the feeling of drowsiness escaped him. He was now wide awake and filled with apprehension. This anxiety grew as the minutes ticked by. Soon he found himself experiencing unexplained waves of fear. Unable to stand it any longer, he was just about to get up from the bed when he heard a rustling noise from within the bathroom. The door creaked open, and out stepped his wife. The man sprang from the bed and looked down in horror at the lump he had assumed was his sleeping wife. The lump had vanished, and the covers now lay smooth and unperturbed on the other side of the bed. Who or what had he been lying next to?

Mirror, Mirror on the Wall

Leslie Heller, a recent manager of the hotel, had this story to tell. One evening, her staff was setting up for dinner in the main dining room. Just to the left of the kitchen door, there hangs a large rectangular mirror with an ornate gold frame. The mirror is quite old, and the glass is wavy, distorting images, as is common with glass produced long ago. While setting up, one waiter stopped to snap a photo of his friends in the dining room. Later that night, when the crew looked at the photo, they saw someone reflected in the corner of that old mirror who had not actually been in the room. Leslie said that in the corner of the mirror there appeared a woman's reflection from the shoulders up. She had short, bobbed hair and an old-fashioned dress with a wide collar. Her face and features were blurred, but the one detail that disturbed the staff the most was the woman's neck. It appeared to be quite long, thin and unnaturally crooked. Now when I was told this story, I immediately shuddered. I had read a clipping from one of the old Creede papers not long before describing the death of a young woman named Mary Spitz.[103] Mary was employed at the Creede Hotel in the late 1920s. She had not worked for the hotel long, when one evening she was given the task of going out back to empty a "waste pot" into the creek. Mary did not return, and the other employees thought she had gone home early with a headache.

This old mirror hangs in the dining room of the Creede Hotel. The Zang's sign above it was found in the attic and brought out for display. *Author collection.*

Her husband said he thought she might have "stayed with a friend" that evening, so he did not report her missing either. Mary's lifeless body was spotted the next morning in the creek at the end of town. She had fallen in and met her death the previous evening. The mysterious visage reflected in the old mirror with her bobbed hair and wide, sailor-like collar certainly seemed characteristic of a young woman from the 1920s. Could the crooked neck have been the result of a break as Mary plunged into and was battered by the rocks in the swiftly flowing Willow Creek?

A Helpful Haunting

During my college years, I spent summers as a waitress working for the Ormsbys at the Creede Hotel. I never saw a ghost myself but often heard them pacing the floors of the presumably empty rooms above the dining room. We were not much afraid of them, but sometimes those raucous spirits did cause the dining room chandelier to tremble. A few of my friends who were also employed at the hotel had more remarkable encounters than I. This is Eryn Wintz's story:

In the mid-1990s, Eryn worked at the hotel for Cathy and Rich as a morning baker. It was one of her many jobs in town that summer, and she would start her day at 4:00 a.m. baking bread in the hotel kitchen. Most times she was the only one on the premises and certainly the only one in the restaurant. One such morning, she had an odd experience as she was finishing up her last tray of homemade potato rolls. She remembers pulling the rolls out of the oven and then stretching on her tiptoes with the pan over her head trying to slide it into the top slot on the otherwise full baking rack. The pan was almost there but teetered not quite far enough in to catch the rim of the baking rack. Just then the hot pan slipped and burned her wrists over the oven mitts. She nearly stepped aside to let it clatter to the floor, when the pan of rolls mysteriously levitated from her grip and slid smoothly into the top slot of that baking rack. Eryn took off the oven mitts, stepped back and said, "Well, thank you!" before hurrying off to her next job of the day baking croissants down the street at Cafe Olé.

A similarly helpful spirit encounter was reported just a few years back when one of the hotel's waitstaff walked toward a closed kitchen door with a precariously stacked armload of dishes. He was just about to call for help when the door suddenly swung open just long enough to allow him to pass safely through. Then it shut neatly behind him, click. There was no one nearby who could have assisted.

It is my belief that the ghost most often encountered at the Creede Hotel is Lizzie Zang Orthen. She certainly loved her hotel, and it would stand to reason that she is still there continuing to watch over things, helping when needed and attempting to communicate with those who work and stay there. The spirit of the old lady with her white hair and long gown could indeed be Lizzie as she appeared at the end of her life. A pair of paranormal researchers came to investigate the Creede Hotel several years ago.[104] They noted electronic voice phenomenon (EVP) and made a digital recording of a series of questions asked of the ghosts. When they asked the names of the spirits at the hotel, one of the answers they received was "Liz."[105] This was reported in their book with no mention of who Liz might have been. I do not believe they knew that they had likely reached out and contacted the hotel's original proprietress. In my opinion, this lends even more credibility to their findings. When they asked how many spirits resided at the Creede Hotel, the answer they heard was "eight."[106] I mentioned this number to Cathy Ormsby, and she replied, "That might just explain all the presences that Rich felt were lined up on the stairs behind the old lady."

My research also turned up some deaths that occurred at the old hotel. On March 7, 1906, J.W. Scott, a former deputy sheriff of Gunnison County, passed away from pneumonia in his room at the Zang.[107] Another heart-wrenching death occurred there in September 1915, when a frantic couple brought their six-month-old baby in to town from Wagon Wheel Gap on a railway handcar. They knew the passenger train was running late and had no time to waste. The sick baby was taken directly to Dr. McKibbin, who diagnosed pneumonia and told the mother and father to "take the baby to a hotel and put it to bed, as he was afraid it was dying." The baby passed away later that day at the Zang Hotel.[108] Could these be a few of the other spirits that haunt the Creede Hotel? Perhaps. Are you brave enough to book a room and find out more for yourself?

6

A CREEDE GHOST IN DEL NORTE

Every love story is a ghost story.
—David Foster Wallace

On April 2, 1906, a poised and beautiful young lady from Creede arrived in Del Norte on the early morning train. She checked into the Windsor Hotel, requesting the finest room. After signing the register with a pseudonym, she left her small traveling case in room 209, strolled down the street and bought a .38-caliber revolver. When the clerk attempted to show her how to clean the revolver, she told him matter-of-factly that she knew as much about guns as he did. Returning to the Windsor, the young beauty, heartbroken and bereft, shut herself away in her richly appointed room. There she wrote two letters, one to her father and the second to her former fiancé, the man who had, only the night before, asked to be released from his promise to marry her. She then wrote a brief note to the hotel's staff.[109]

Not long after, two shots rang through the cold morning air. The room clerk who happened to be tidying the room adjacent rushed downstairs, found the cook and exclaimed that she was afraid the girl in the next room had just shot herself. The cook ran up the stairs and burst into the room arriving only seconds before the young lady took her last gasping breath. She had shot herself, the paper reported, through the lower ventricle of her heart.[110] The note she left for the Windsor staff explained that her real name was Maud Heinz and asked that her father, Charles Heinz of Creede,

LOST LOVER GAINS DEATH

Young Woman Jilted Sits By Bed and Sends a Bullet Into Her Breast.

ROMANCE ENDS BY GRAVE

Herald Democrat headline, April 3, 1906. *Colorado Historic Newspapers online.*

be notified, along with V.W. Parker of Chama.[111] Thus begins the tale of how Maud Heinz's spirit came to haunt the Windsor Hotel.

When I phoned the Windsor one afternoon, I was put in touch with a gentleman who I was told would be a reliable source regarding the haunting. He has been involved with the Windsor Hotel restoration and renovation for years and told me that he does not consider the Windsor a haunted hotel. He says there are rarely any strange events or ghostly happenings, despite its history. Rarely, however, does not mean never. He described a time when there was more spiritual activity at the hotel, and a series of strange and inexplicable events occurred. There was a period, he explained, when the hotel was run by proprietors who had a rather tumultuous relationship and often bitterly quarreled at work. He believed this turmoil upset the spirits. Guests reported hearing commotion in the hallways in the late night and early morning hours, televisions snapped on and off by themselves and glasses flew from the bar shelves, shattering on the floor. Guests in room 209 heard horrible moans that would end abruptly when the light was switched on, and some even saw the ethereal figure of a woman floating near their bed.[112]

Later, when this man and his family took over management of the hotel, they attempted to communicate with Maud's spirit. They took a big bouquet of flowers up to room 209 and left them on the bedside table. "Maud, we know this is your home, and we respect that. All that we ask is that you please not frighten our guests." This lovely gesture seemed to work—at least for a time. As mentioned previously, there is very little paranormal activity reported at the Windsor these days. That does not mean that Maud has vacated the premises. Paranormal events are still reported from time to time, and they seem to happen to people least likely to expect them. I was told that the Windsor has hosted two government agents on a regular basis over several years. It was only after about two years of seeing the ghost that these two agents felt comfortable enough with the proprietor to share their experiences. They saw Maud every single time they stayed at the Windsor. They never knew where or when she would appear, but she was sure to do so at some point each time they came. Sometimes she would be staring out at them as they passed a lonely and darkened room; other times she would be standing in the corner of the room if they awoke in the night. Understandably, it made them considerably uncomfortable, if not a little terrified. The agents' story was shared with a friend of the proprietor, and she recommended that he advise the gentlemen to simply tell her on their next sighting, "Maud, please do not appear to us anymore. You are scaring us." The advice was followed, and the agents have not since encountered Maud.

I have heard that some guests who are particularly sensitive to such things tell of an overwhelming feeling of despair and sadness when they are on the second floor of the Windsor. One woman described being inexplicably flooded by memories of her own first love and the devastation of their parting. She said she had not thought of this boy in years and reported that being engulfed in the nostalgia was rather bittersweet and not altogether an unpleasant experience. Another guest recalled being gently roused from sleep one evening by the haunting notes of a melancholic tune being played on a far-off violin. She listened for a moment and then drifted back to sleep.

But who was Maud Heinz and what brought her to the Windsor on the that fateful spring morning in 1906? Maud was twenty-six years old, and according to the U.S. Census Bureau, the average age for a woman to marry in that era was about twenty-one and a half years old. She was an accomplished musician, gifted at both the piano and the violin. "Her character was above reproach and she was popular with a great number of people in the valley, but especially in Creede."[113] She came to Creede as a child of ten during the very early days of the silver boom. Maud was the third of six children. She had two sisters: one older, Nettie, and one younger, Norine. She had three brothers: Charley, the eldest of all the Heinz children, and Langley and Orel, both younger than Maud. One of the earliest mentions of her in the *Creede Candle* describes a party Maud attended, whiling away the afternoon hours playing hearts with her friends.[114] Other mentions of Maud refer to her talent and activities as a musician: she traveled to Alamosa to play in an orchestra for the Leap Year dance, performed a violin solo at a celebration held by the Women of Woodcraft in Creede and received this compliment, "Her renditions on the violin are equal to the best."[115] In his memoir, *Boom Town Boy in Old Creede, Colorado*, Edwin Lewis Bennett reminisced about many pleasant evenings spent dancing at the Derrick Hall to the music of the Heinz Orchestra. "The Derrick," as they called it, once stood in the now vacant lot at the end of Fourth Street, between the railroad tracks and Rio

Popular Broadway star Viola Allen, circa 1903. According to one source, Maud used the pseudonym Viola Allen when she signed into the Windsor Hotel on the morning of her suicide. *Library of Congress.*

Grande Avenue (also known in Creede as "the back street"). Bennett recalled listening to "the Heinz Orchestra, with Charles on cornet and Maud and Nettie on violin and piano. What their orchestra lacked in size it made up in sweetness of music and perfect time."[116] The pseudonym Maud used when signing into the Windsor that sad day was reported differently by two papers, one printing that she signed in as "Violet Tierri" and the other reporting the pseudonym to have been "Viola Allen."[117] Both papers noted that she gave her city of residence as Columbus, Ohio, her father's hometown.[118] Violet Tierri seems to be a whimsical name she might have created, but if she did indeed use the name Viola Allen, she was borrowing the name of a famous Broadway actress of the time. Allen was a celebrated Shakespearean actress on the Great White Way. An artist herself, it is likely that Maud knew of and admired Viola Allen.

It is uncertain how Maud met and became engaged to V.W. Parker, but given that he worked as a brakeman for the Denver and Rio Grande Railway (D&RGR), it is likely that they met through her brother Charley, also a brakeman for the D&RGR.[119] Parker and Maud became engaged on New Year's Day 1906, beginning the New Year with a champagne toast and an engagement announcement. Maud likely did not know that Parker had recently ended another engagement after quarreling with Miss Gertrude Walker. A few months later, in late March, he ran into Miss Walker in Alamosa. The couple settled their differences, and Parker decided that Gertrude was the one he wanted to marry. Later that same day, he explained the situation to Maud and asked to be released from his engagement to her. According to the *San Juan Prospector*, Maud appeared to take the news well: "[She] consented, saying that if he loved Miss Walker better than he did her, she would not hold him to his promise."[120] The next morning, Maud traveled to the Windsor to end her heartbreak by literally tearing her own heart in two.

A family friend told the *San Juan Prospector* that Maud had suffered a head injury in a "runaway accident" only two years prior to her death. It was not explained further, but most likely, a runaway horse threw Maud or she fell from a carriage being pulled by a runaway horse. This accident left Maud unconscious for over two hours, and as a result, she suffered from headaches and "visionary spells." Perhaps to lessen the blow of her suicide on the family, this friend speculated that this accident "might account for her grieving over the breaking off of an engagement."[121] Mr. Heinz, "nearly prostrated with grief," appeared later that day to collect his daughter's body and return it to Creede.[122]

Maud's father, Charles Heinz, was one of the first on the boomtown scene, arriving in Creede with his family in 1890.[123] He built and opened the Bimetallic Exchange, also known by many as merely the "Heinz Saloon." This saloon was in the two-story Heinz Building, which sat on the corner of Main and Wall Streets in what was then called Jimtown.

The Heinz Building later burned to the ground in January 1936. It stood where the Creede Trading Post is now. Many will be surprised to learn that Creede's most beloved antique bar, the one that currently stands with stately grace in the back room of the Creede Historical Museum in the old depot, was originally a fixture at Heinz's Bimetallic Exchange. The bar came to the saloon around the turn of the century as a promotion given away by a Milwaukee beer company. In 1905, Heinz purchased Antler's Ranch. He moved his family from their home on the mesa out to the ranch and began the daunting job of managing both ranch and saloon. Sometime after Maud's tragic death, Heinz's health began to fail. After a prolonged illness, he passed away in 1913 at the age of only fifty-seven. The headline in the *Creede Candle* read, "Another Creede Pioneer Dead."[124] The old bar was sold to another saloon keeper across the street. In 1940, the bar again changed hands after being auctioned off on Main Street. It

BIMETALLIC EXCHANGE

Fine Wines, Liquors
and Cigars . . .

CHAS. HEINZ, Prop

Left: Charles Heinz's Bimetallic Exchange Advertisement, 1907. *From the* Creede Candle, *Colorado Historic Newspapers online.*

Below: Muleskinners load and unload freight from their mules near the depot. Charles Heinz's Bimetallic Saloon is in the center. *Creede Historical Society Archives.*

The grave of Maud Heinz can be found in Creede's cemetery on the hill above town.
Photograph by Bob Seago.

was then moved up to the Rainbo Cafe (later called the Golden Nugget) in the space now occupied by the Del Norte Bank. The bar would remain in the Nugget for many years. In 1985, it was sold out of town, but happily, only five years later the Creede Historical Society was able to purchase the bar and return it to its rightful home in Creede.[125]

Maud Heinz was buried in the Creede Cemetery on April 4, 1906, two days after her tragic suicide. The reporter for the *San Juan Prospector* wrote that "the burial ended what might have been a brilliant career and a bright future."[126] Maud's tombstone, erected by the Women of Woodcraft, can still be found in the cemetery on the hill overlooking Creede. In winter, it is encrusted with ice and snow and in summer entangled in wildflowers. Perhaps you can find time one day to locate this old grave and leave a flower for Maud Heinz, nearly forgotten by the citizens of Creede but well remembered in Del Norte as the ghost that haunts the Windsor Hotel.

7

A GHOST IS SUMMONED
TO THE STAGE

I can call spirits from the vasty deep.
Why, so can I, or so can any man;
But will they come when you do call for them?
—*William Shakespeare,* Henry IV, Part I

Originally built in the 1930s as a movie theater, the building that now houses the Creede Repertory Theatre (CRT) has seen many improvements and renovations over the last ninety years and would hardly be recognizable to those who first erected it. During the 1950s, it hosted an amateur melodrama complete with can-can girls, and in 1966, Operation Summer Theatre was created by the Creede JayCees and JayCee-ettes, bringing twelve students from the University of Kansas to town to produce plays during the summer months. The operation grew and changed, and CRT is now one of the largest employers in Mineral County during the summer months. The company has received many accolades and awards, and audience members enjoy shows here from May through September each year.

Theaters are often known for their ghost stories, and most of CRT's ghosts seem to reside at the boardinghouse, the old Rio Grande Hotel, affectionately known as "the bordello." I'll tell you more of those tales later. The theater itself does have a ghost story though, centered on the two second-story bedrooms that were once above the lobby/box office area and behind the balcony. Directors and designers were often housed in these rooms, and many would complain of being kept awake by loud parties that raged into the early morning hours next door at the Creede Hotel bar. Disheveled and grumpy from lack of sleep, these fatigued artists would voice their displeasure the next day about being kept up by all of the ruckus, only to learn that it had been a slow night at "the Hotey" (as it was referred to in those days) and the bar had closed early in the evening. These phantom parties that fill the night air with their ghostly gaiety have been reported by many people over the years.

Another more frightening ghost story began one summer evening in 2006 when the talented actress Annie Butler was preparing for a show. That night, she was performing in CRT's production of the play *The Man Who Shot the Man Who Shot Jesse James*. The script brings to life a few of Creede's earliest and most infamous characters, including Jesse James's murderer Bob Ford, Ed O'Kelley and a notorious dancer, played by Annie. That evening, Annie must have been a striking figure as she strolled out on to the small walk bridge spanning Willow Creek just behind the theater. In her full costume, a floor-length black Victorian gown complete with lace, puffed sleeves and a bustle, she began her vocal warm-ups as the sun slipped down behind the mountain and faded from the cliffs above her. She stood over Willow Creek, and suddenly, filled with inspiration, she spun to the north, facing up the narrow canyon. Tilting her head back and taking in the majesty of the cliffs, she spread her arms wide and beckoned in a

Above and opposite: Annie Butler and cast perform in the Creede Repertory Theatre's production of *The Man Who Shot the Man Who Shot Jesse James*. *Photograph by John Gary Brown, Creede Repertory Theatre Archives.*

Right: Annie Butler dances onstage in the Creede Repertory Theatre's production of *The Man Who Shot the Man Who Shot Jesse James*. *Photograph by John Gary Brown, Creede Repertory Theatre Archives.*

booming voice, "Spirits of Creede, join me on stage tonight!" The cool air vibrated, and the clear note of her words hung like a charm over the swiftly flowing waters below.

As Annie reentered the theater and took her place in the wings, she felt a growing anticipation and excitement about the show to come. How might the spirits make their presence known? Darkness fell as the first blackout encompassed the house and then the stage. But the show went on as usual without a hitch and was rather uneventful. Annie recalled being a bit disappointed that none of Creede's specters had taken the opportunity to make their stage debut that evening. She had been so sure that she'd made some kind of connection when she'd reached out to the ghosts. It was only when she'd changed out of her costume and started alone down Main Street on her evening trek home in the dark, moonless night that she began to regret her invocation. She immediately had the sensation that someone, or some *thing*, was following her. The feeling grew as she quickened her pace and intensified even more when she turned down the side street to her home. Instead of feeling safe as she rushed into her house and bolted the door behind her, she felt terror. She knew at once that the entity, whatever she had called forth from those dark running waters of Willow Creek, was now inside her home, and panic rose in her breast. Suddenly she found herself pinned against the wall by unseen icy hands. She was released and fell to the floor, struggling against the entity to regain her footing. Pinioned to the ground now, she tried to wrestle free as she fought for her breath. For nearly an hour, Annie battled against the abuse of this entity with its terrifyingly physical presence. At last, she managed to break free and ran to scoop up her small dog and cat that had both been cowering in a corner. She bolted outside and scrambled into her truck. At last, a feeling of safety settled over her. She slept.

For nearly a week, Annie was haunted in the night by the spirit. It refused to allow her any sleep. Finally, at her wits end, she called on Creede's local exorcist, a woman recognized as a healer who had also become known for the ability to get rid of unwanted spirits. This woman asked Annie to please stay outside while she confronted the spirit, asking it to leave. This woman later reported that she found the presence lurking in the shower and that this particular spirit was the most difficult she had ever encountered. While she did not disclose her methods, she was successful in communicating with the entity and sending it back whence it had come. Annie, her small dog and cat were then free to return to their home and have not been forced to sleep in the truck since.

In an interesting twist, I later learned that paranormal researchers often observe that spirits are attracted to or are more likely to materialize near running water. Some believe that these entities draw their energy from the moving water. When Annie stood over Willow Creek and beckoned the spirits to come forth, she greatly increased the power of that invocation. What exactly did she bring forth from the "vasty deep" of Willow Creek? It was certainly not one of the benign spirits of Creede that answered her call. I think we can all learn a valuable lesson from this tale. Never ask for something that you are not certain you want. There were several moments while writing this book when I, stymied by writer's block, felt inclined to call on the spirits of Creede for inspiration. Remembering this tale, I refrained.

8

THE HAUNTED HOUSES

All houses wherein men have lived and died
Are haunted houses. Through the open doors
The harmless phantoms on their errands glide,
With feet that make no sound upon the floors.
—from Haunted Houses *by Henry Wadsworth Longfellow*

MR. TINGLEY

When Iris Birdsey first told me that the ghost that haunted her house was named Mr. Tingley, I laughed. What could be a better name for a ghost? "Did you come up with that one?" I asked. "No," she said. "That's his name, his real name." Mr. Tingley, it turns out, was an actual resident of Creede back in the 1920s. He operated a sawmill and had other (perhaps more lucrative, as you shall see) side projects, and his home was a small cabin on West Sixth Street that sat on the northern end of the lot that Iris and Rocky's house now occupies. According to author John LaFont, Tingley was quite a character:

> *Bill Tingley was another unusual type. He was a pretty burly, tough fellow and a natural logger and saw miller. His sawmill was set up above Marshall Park, or what was sometimes called Whiskey Park....He used*

to supplement his income from the sawmill by running a still and selling whiskey. Marshall Park was one of the favorite camping spots for the summer visitors in the area and there were usually quite a number of them camped there. Tingley got acquainted with some of the campers and let it be known that he had whiskey to sell. This was during prohibition and the illegal product had several names, such as, hootch, rotgut, firewater, moonshine, bootleg, booze and whitemule. Tingley made a little sign and put it up where his road left the county road. On the sign he had an arrow pointing toward his sawmill and the sign read, "Mule for sale." Everybody in the country knew what it meant and this accounted for the name "Whiskey Park."[127]

Iris can verify that Bill Tingley has not given up his idiosyncrasies in the afterlife. It seems Mr. Tingley is a prankster, and one of his favorite tricks is to click the latch and lock the door behind someone who has just left the Birdsey home without a key. He is also fond of hiding objects—important objects. Iris told me that he once hid her husband Rocky's wallet. They knew that the wallet had to be somewhere in the house because that's where it had last been seen. After searching every room for the wallet, Iris and Rocky were at a loss. Finally, they gave up the search and went to bed. The next morning when they awoke, they found the wallet lying smack dab in the center of the kitchen table. When the Birdseys first moved into their home, Iris recalled she would often hear the toilet lid in the bathroom banging up and down. She'd run to the back to see what was causing the commotion, but there would be nothing amiss. She told her in-laws, Sam and Garnet Birdsey, about this strange phenomenon, and they laughed. She swore it was the truth but had a hard time convincing anyone until one night when she had her in-laws over for dinner. After dinner, they were all playing cards, and the toilet lid began to bang up and down in the back. "That! That's what I've been trying to tell you about." Iris exclaimed. Garnet immediately got to her feet and walked to the back to see what could be making that racket. The noise stopped. Garnet returned and sat back down at the table. "There's no one back there, and I have no idea what was making that noise," she reported. At that point, Sam looked up from his cards and said, "Oh, there's nothing to worry about. That's just old Mr. Tingley. He never had plumbing, and he's trying to figure out what that contraption is in the middle of his cabin!" Everyone at the table had a good laugh at that. I'm just wondering if Mr. Tingley was trying to figure out if that "contraption" could be used for making moonshine.

THE PARLOR HOUSE

Directly across West Sixth Street from the Birdseys' residence is one of Creede's oldest homes. Sam Birdsey, born in Creede in 1907 and a lifelong resident, always said that this house across the street had once been a "cat house," or brothel; he also insisted that the old Rio Grande Hotel, which everyone now calls "the bordello," was never any such thing. It's not hard to imagine this pretty little house on the corner, now painted white with blue trim, was once a parlor house. A lovely little anecdote from Edwin Lewis Bennett's memoir *Boom Town Boy* confirmed for me that this house was indeed a parlor house and even solved the mystery of who ran it:

> *After all the arrivals on the morning train had gone and I was the only one left of the local yokels who, for lack of anything better to do, had met the train, there was still on the platform a good-looking woman who was somewhere in her late twenties. At her feet were two small suitcases and she had been looking around as though someone should be there.*
>
> *"Were you expecting to be met?" I asked her.*
>
> *"Yes, I was," she answered, "but nobody has shown up."*
>
> *"Glad to help if I can," I told her. "I could carry your suitcases if you know where to go."*
>
> *"Oh," she said, "I know where I'm going but you don't."*
>
> *"It isn't a very big town," I argued, "and if those suitcases aren't any heavier than they look, I'm sure I could carry them to the city limits in any direction and still come out alive."*
>
> *"But I'm going to Lillis's," she said, "if you know where that is."*
>
> *I had begun to suspect as much so was not surprised. I told her I had seen the place, occasionally and from a distance, and knew where it was. "It's not far and all downhill so let's go." Together we walked down Rio Grande Avenue that would lead us to Sixth.*
>
> *As we turned the corner toward her future residence, she said she would like to offer to pay me but she was so broke she was afraid I might take it and she couldn't afford that. Over her almost determined refusal, I lent her ten dollars that represented practically all my capital.*
>
> *"All right," she finally agreed, "I'm so strapped ten dollars looks like a million to me and I'll pay it back just a soon as I can." After a moment, she added, "In cash." And she did.*[128]

According to one old-timer, this old house was once a brothel, likely run by "Creede Lil."
Author collection.

The Lillis that Bennett referred to is Lillis Lovell, better known by many as Creede's queen of easy virtue, the beautiful madam "Creede Lil." Originally from Nebraska, Lil's real name was Emma Lillis Quigley.[129] Lil was reportedly a well-known opera singer who made a rather drastic change in her career path. Throughout her second career she worked in Leadville, Cripple Creek, Creede and finally Denver. It seems that most of her career was spent running the house on West Sixth Street in Creede. She is listed on a 1900 Creede census as head of the household, thirty-five years of age, owning her home and residing with three boarders: twenty-year-old Trissi, thirty-four-year-old Gladys and twenty-three-year-old Bulah. Perhaps one of these ladies was even the one assisted by a young Bennett. All the women listed their occupation as prostitute. It must not have been too long after the census was taken that Creede Lil moved to Denver, where she married banker Clarence J. Trimble in 1901.[130] She ran a house in Denver's Tenderloin Resort at 2020 Market Street for a time but died of pneumonia in March 1907 at the age of only forty-two.[131]

Above: Gentlemen wait for the train along the back platform of the Jimtown depot. *Al Birdsey Collection, Creede Historical Society Archives.*

Right: Popular Creede madam Lillis Lovell, known to most as "Creede Lil." *Courtesy of the Old Homestead House Museum, Cripple Creek, Colorado.*

There are a few ghost stories associated with the old house that was once Creede Lil's parlor house. I remember going to Girl Scout meetings there as a child. Yvonne Hosselkus was one of our troop leaders, and her husband, Sonny, was fond of telling us spooky stories. We were easily scared, and he loved telling the tales as much as we enjoyed hearing them. The one I remember most had to do with the old laundry chute and how laundry and other sundry items would often come down this chute when there was no one upstairs to have sent them down. It was presumed that the ghost was up there sorting the laundry. Later, as the troop settled in and began to recite the Girl Scout pledge, several items could be heard tumbling down the laundry chute from upstairs. We all screamed and fled the room.

Liz Curry, who grew up in the house, had a frightening encounter with a ghost one evening as she was trying to get to sleep. She remembered climbing into bed and then feeling that she was being watched by a male presence from the corner of her room. The feeling was so overpowering that she was frozen with dread and unable to get up or even call out to her siblings and parents. She pulled the quilt over her head and quaked under the covers until, finally, filled with terror and exhausted, she dropped off to sleep. The next morning, Liz awoke with her head still buried under the quilt. She was relieved to see the sun beginning to filter in through her curtains, so she cautiously lowered the quilt and got out of bed. When she turned to look down at her quilt, she was horrified to see muddy boot prints from the foot of the bed all the way up to the headboard, as if the ghost had walked right over her and exited through the wall in the middle of the night.

THE RIO GRANDE HOTEL

The Rio Grande Hotel at 209 West Second Street was built in 1892 during the height of Creede's boom by the Denver and Rio Grande Railway and was used primarily to house employees. It was then sold to Daniel L. Motz and converted into a single-family home around 1900.[132] Motz and his family had arrived in Creede in 1891 and operated a shoe store, their motto being, "If they don't suit you, don't take them."[133] The large family occupied the house for several generations. Motz passed away in the house in March 1914 after a two-month illness.[134] He was seventy-four. His wife had preceded him in death in 1911, and his daughter Zula Motz Wheeler followed in 1918 at the age of only forty-four.[135] Zula's husband, Theodore Wheeler, and

View of downtown Creede, circa late 1892 or early 1893. The depot is under construction, and the Rio Grande Hotel can be seen along the hillside with a false front square façade. The road to the left of the hotel would later become the sledding hill. *Creede Historical Society Archives.*

their six children resided in the house for many years, until, according to a relative, the upkeep and maintenance became too much and they moved to a smaller home next door. For many years, the old Rio Grande Hotel sat abandoned and neglected there on the hillside, sliding into terrible disrepair. It was purchased and restored to some extent in the 1970s and then sold again to the Creede Repertory Theatre in 1983. It was at this time that the nickname "the bordello" was given to the old hotel, as Jan Jacobs, a CRT board member at the time, recalled that the interior had been decorated in quite a gaudy manner, with gold flocked wallpaper, crystal chandeliers and red velvet curtains reminiscent of a turn-of-the-century bordello. The theater still uses the old hotel as a boardinghouse for summer company members, and in 2000, a complete renovation and restoration project was initiated. A State Historical Fund grant was awarded to the project and used to spark a fundraising campaign that was leveraged into over $1 million for the entire project.[136] The restored hotel still has its ghosts though.

While there are several ghost stories associated with the old hotel, one of my favorites dates to the 1940s. A former superintendent of the Creede Schools told me this tale. It occurred one snowy and overcast day when he

The Rio Grande Hotel now serves as a boardinghouse for Creede Repertory Theatre employees. *Author collection.*

was a small boy of about eight. A group of kids gathered that morning at the sledding hill to play. The sledding hill at that time (and even as late as the 1980s) was on an old road that ran down from the mesa just south of the Rio Grande Hotel, and the sleds came to a stop at the base of that road near the old hotel.

After sledding for about an hour, a group of the older kids began to grow bored. They decided that everyone should leave their sleds at the foot of the hill and sneak into the old hotel to explore. None of the younger kids wanted any part of this plan. The rumor, of course, and general consensus was that the old hotel was haunted, and the overcast day made it appear even drearier than usual. The older kids were insistent, however, that everyone must come. It took much convincing and some questioning of bravery, but in the end, all the kids made their way through the snow and over to the side door of the hotel. One older boy turned the doorknob, and to everyone's surprise, the door creaked open and swung inward. The bigger kids led the way, slowly creeping along the entryway and into the front parlor with a small group of younger children lagging behind on the porch in trepidation. The storyteller told me that he believed that the older kids had a plan all along for scaring the younger ones once they were inside, but that plan was about to be thwarted.

As the oldest boy crossed into the front parlor, the timeworn player piano that stood in the corner abruptly began to crank out a tune. The notes filled the frozen room, the music roll spun and the floor pedals of the piano jerked up and down, striking terror in the hearts of all present. One child shrieked, and everyone scrambled to get out of the house—the older kids knocking down the smaller ones in their frantic race out the door.

In the summer of 1992, after a particularly late technical rehearsal, many of the CRT company members, myself included, gathered across the street at the Old Miners Inn (OMI) saloon. One intern happened to be particularly exhausted and headed home to the bordello after only one beer. When he got back to the bordello, he realized he was completely alone in the old house for the first time ever. Feeling somewhat unsettled, he climbed the narrow flight of steps to his room at the top of the stairs, opened the door and flicked on the light. The light illuminated an old rocking chair in the corner of the room, and much to his surprise, it was wildly creaking and rocking back and forth. My friend flew down the stairs and sprinted back to the OMI, where he told our table of friends what had happened. He said, "I've either had too much to drink or not enough." Well, we ordered him a shot, and he vowed never to return to the bordello alone again.

He's not the only one to have something spooky happen in that particular room. Another pair of occupants of the room at the top of the stairs complained of their clock radio switching on every morning at 3:00 a.m. They unplugged it, and still, at precisely 3:00 a.m., static began to blare from the radio. The next morning, the batteries were removed, so they felt sure that there would be nothing to awake them at 3:00 a.m. When the radio alarm clicked on that next morning at 3:00 a.m., it was thrown out the window by the terrified roommates.

An actress who stayed in the same room reported that every night she would go to sleep only to awaken in terror with the sensation of something sitting or pressing on her chest, making it extremely difficult to breathe. After a little research, she learned that the phenomenon of the chest-sitting ghost is reported in different cultures throughout the world and that sometimes such a ghost has a message it is trying to relay to the living. The actress felt certain that there had to be some significance to these nightly visits. She also had the feeling that the spirit was female. After some soul searching, this young lady decided that the ghost did not like her boyfriend. She knew herself that he was not the best fit for her and did not treat her well. After she broke things off with him, she never again experienced those ghostly night terrors of someone pressing on her chest.

Another resident of the bordello reported being awakened in the middle of the night by a panicked voice screaming her name repeatedly, only to find the entire house pitch black with no other living soul stirring. Doors and windows throughout the house are known to fly open or slam shut on their own as the spirits travel about at their leisure. The bordello ghosts make their presence known every summer.

THE DWYER HOUSE

According to the Creede Historical Society, this two-story clapboard home is the oldest house in Creede that is still in the family of the original owner. You can find it just over the walk bridge on East Fourth Street, behind the Creede Community Church. The Dwyers were some of the first residents of the Creede camp, and one of the home's early occupants was at one time supervisor of the Commodore Mine on West Willow. Story has it that the back part of the house was moved by wagon to Creede from Tres Piedras, New Mexico, in the southern end of the San Luis Valley.[137]

The Dwyer house is one of Creede's oldest homes. *Author collection.*

The little red house has, for as long as I can remember, had a ghost story associated with it. As a child, I recall hurrying past it on my way to the grocery store or another errand. My eyes strangely drawn to it, I would examine the windows closely, hoping, dreading and nearly certain that one day I would see someone or something peering back at me from behind the lacy curtains.

When I began to collect specific stories for my ghost tour, I realized that I had never actually heard "the story" behind the haunted red house. I emailed my high school English teacher John Goss, whose family still owns the house, and he agreed to meet and tell me the tale, although he warned me that it might not be what I was expecting.

When John Goss first moved to Creede to teach English at the high school during the 1970s, he lived in the old family home that had been passed down from generation to generation and now belonged to his mother. His students often asked him if the old house was haunted, and he refused to confirm or deny anything. Of course, his silence only fueled the imaginations of the kids who were already convinced that the old house must have its ghosts. The time came when John knew that he would be getting married and moving out of the old house and into a newer and less drafty one. Realizing that the house would be standing empty, he decided he might want to conjure up a few sightings of the "ghost of Uncle Martin," a family member who had lived in the home long ago. He felt that a resident ghost might spook away any miscreants motivated to break in to the soon-to-be-empty house. Apparently just the suggestion that the house was haunted did indeed keep it safe over the years. The ghostly tale gained some notoriety when it was mentioned in the *Historic Creede, A Walking Tour* brochure published by the Creede Historical Society.

Not everyone in John's family was happy with his whimsical tales of Uncle Martin's ghost, however. John reports being scolded by his mother, who was quite displeased with the notion that any of her relatives would return to haunt the old house instead of resting peacefully in the hereafter. It's worth noting that John has two sisters who do believe there is a ghost haunting the Dwyer house, so I may yet one day see a spectral face gazing out from behind those lace curtains.

A SPIRITED FAREWELL

Thank you for joining me on this haunted journey through the pages of Creede's storied past. I hope you have enjoyed these tales and learned a little history along the way. And as for these Creede ghosts, I'd like to believe that most of them are not really trapped here. These spirits know as well as the rest of us that Creede is a little piece of heaven, and this is where they choose to remain. As the *Creede Candle* tells us Lizzie Zang Orthen once exclaimed upon returning to Creede from an extended six-week trip to visit relatives, "There is no place exactly like Creede!"[138] I have to agree.

Creede, Colorado, December 1942. Library of Congress; photograph by Andreas Feininger.

Notes

Introduction

1. Wolle, *Stampede to Timberline*, 319.
2. Horn, "Brunot Agreement."
3. Ibid.
4. Wolle, *Stampede to Timberline*, 320.
5. Ibid., 322.

Chapter 1

6. Wagner and Wetherill, *Hidden History*, 163.
7. Ibid., 165.
8. Ibid., 162; LaFont, *Homesteaders*, 54.
9. *Colorado Daily Chieftain*, September 4, 1875.
10. LaFont, *Homesteaders*, 54.
11. Ibid.
12. Wagner and Wetherill, *Hidden History*, 165.
13. LaFont, *Homesteaders*, 54.
14. Ibid.
15. *Silver Thread Summer Guide*, 1992.
16. History Nebraska, "Rough on Rats, and Biles and Piles and Corns," https://history.nebraska.gov.

Chapter 2

17. *Mineral County Miner*, October 29, 2009.
18. *Creede Candle*, April 12, 1892.
19. Feitz, *Quick History of Creede*, 23.
20. Smith, *Alias Soapy Smith*, 245.
21. Feitz, *Soapy Smith's Creede*, 3.
22. Feitz, *Quick History of Creede*, 19.
23. *Creede Candle*, February 18, 1892.
24. Cooper, "Easy Come, Easy Go."
25. *Colorado Daily Chieftain*, March 2, 1895.
26. Smith, *Alias, Soapy Smith*, 235.
27. Ibid., 243.
28. Ibid., 244.
29. Ye Olde Curiosity Shop, "Sylvester."
30. Smith, *Alias Soapy Smith*, 244–45.
31. Ibid., 243.
32. Donovan, "Ye Olde Curiosity Shop."

Chapter 3

33. *Creede Candle*, April 22, 1892.
34. Mumey, *Creede*, 142.
35. *Colorado Daily Chieftain*, June 13, 1892.
36. Clark, *Bob Ford*, 22.
37. Cooper, "Easy Come, Easy Go."
38. Clark, *Bob Ford*, 17.
39. Braiden, "Early Days," 46–47.
40. *Creede Candle*, March 7, 1914, and March 14, 1914.
41. Ibid., September 11, 1909.
42. *Salida Mail*, July 12, 1892.
43. Clark, *Bob Ford*, 25–26.

Chapter 4

44. *San Juan Prospector*, May 23, 1891.
45. *Colorado Daily Chieftain*, May 6, 1892.

46. *Gunnison Daily News-Democrat*, March 23, 1882.

47. *Salida Mail*, July 26, 1884.

48. Ibid.

49. Ibid.

50. Ibid., February 11, 1887.

51. *San Juan Prospector*, May 23, 1891.

52. Ibid., August 1, 1891

53. *Colorado Daily Chieftain*, May 6, 1892.

54. *Creede Candle*, January 14, 1892.

55. *Colorado Daily Chieftain*, May 6, 1892.

56. Mumey, *Creede*. 142.

57. Ibid., May 6,1892; *San Juan Prospector*, November 7, 1891.

58. *San Juan Prospector*, November 7, 1891.

59. Ibid.

60. Ibid.

61. *Creede Candle*, May 6, 1892.

62. Ibid., November 21, 1891.

63. Ibid., November 28, 1891, and January 7, 1892.

64. *Saguache Crescent*, May 11, 1893.

65. *Creede Candle*, November 7, 1891.

66. Buchanan and Jacobs, *Historic Creede, A Walking Tour*.

67. *Creede Candle*, January 7, 1892.

68. *Littleton Independent*, May 14, 1892.

69. Ibid.

70. Mumey, *Creede*, 111.

71. *Creede Candle*, May 6, 1892.

72. Ibid.

73. *Colorado Daily Chieftain*, May 6, 1892.

74. *Littleton Independent*, May 14, 1892.

75. *Creede Candle*, May 6, 1892.

76. *Boulder Daily Camera*, May 7, 1892.

77. *Rocky Mountain News*, May 7, 1892.

78. *Creede Candle*, May 13, 1892.

79. Ibid.

80. Ibid.

81. Mumey, *Creede*, 115.

82. *Aspen Daily Leader*, May 25, 1892.

83. Ibid.

84. Ibid.

85. Ibid.
86. *Aspen Daily Times*, May 25, 1892.

Chapter 5

87. *Creede Candle*, June 17, 1911.
88. Ibid.
89. Ibid.
90. Ibid., July 5, 1892, and July 29, 1892.
91. Ibid., April 20, 1894, and April 27, 1894.
92. Ibid., August 29, 1908.
93. Ibid., November 7, 1908.
94. Ibid., May 13, 1905.
95. Ibid., March 18, 1905.
96. Ibid., December 17, 1910.
97. Ibid., June 17, 1911.
98. Ibid.
99. Ibid.
100. Ibid., June 24, 1911.
101. Ibid., November 29, 1919.
102. Ibid., April 30, 1921.
103. Creede Pioneer Society Record, Colorado Historical Society Archive, 31.
104. Todd and O'Connell-Todd, *Wild West Ghosts*, 28.
105. Ibid., 30.
106. Ibid., 29.
107. *Creede Candle*, March 10, 1906.
108. Ibid., September 11, 1915.

Chapter 6

109. *San Juan Prospector*, April 7, 1906.
110. Ibid.
111. Ibid.
112. Williams, *Haunted Hotels of Southern Colorado*.
113. *San Juan Prospector*, April 7, 1906.
114. *Creede Candle*, July 29, 1905.
115. *Alamosa Journal*, June 4, 1903.

116. Bennett and Spring, *Boom Town Boy*, 27.

117. *San Juan Prospector*, April 7, 1906; *Herald Democrat*, April 3, 1906.

118. *Creede Candle*, December 20, 1913.

119. Ibid., November 6, 1909.

120. *San Juan Prospector*, April 7, 1906.

121. Ibid.

122. Ibid.

123. *Creede Candle*, December 20, 1913.

124. Ibid.

125. Buchanan, *Creede Historical Society Museum Self-Guided Tour*.

126. *San Juan Prospector*, April 7, 1906.

Chapter 8

127. LaFont, *58 Years Around Creede*, 104.

128. Bennett and Spring, *Boom Town Boy*, 144–45.

129. Mackall, *Bordellos, Brothels & Bad Girls*, 96.

130. Ibid.

131. Ibid.

132. History Colorado, "Rio Grande Hotel."

133. *Creede Candle*, December 9, 1905.

134. Ibid., March 27, 1914.

135. Ibid., November 9, 1918.

136. History Colorado, "Rio Grande Hotel."

137. Buchanan and Jacobs, *Historic Creede, A Walking Tour*.

Afterword—A Spirited Farewell

138. *Creede Candle*, March 24, 1923.

BIBLIOGRAPHY

Bennett, Edwin Lewis, and Agnes Wright Spring. *Boom Town Boy in Old Creede, Colorado*. Chicago: Swallow Press, 1966.

Blair, Kay Reynolds. *Ladies of the Lamplight*. Ouray, CO: Western Reflections Publishing Company, 2004.

Braiden, William A., as told to Irma S. Harvey. "Early Days in the San Luis Valley." *Colorado Magazine* 21, no. 2 (March 1944).

Buchanan, Lucille. *Creede Historical Society Museum Self-Guided Tour*. Creede Historical Society, Inc. Revised 2017.

Buchanan, Lucille, and Janis Jacobs. *Historic Creede, A Walking Tour*. Creede Historical Society, revised May 2007.

Clark, David W. *Bob Ford: Jesse James' Killer Shot Down in Creede*. Creede, CO: Creede Historical Society Inc., 2015.

Colorado Historic Newspapers Collection. www.coloradohistoricnewspapers.org.

Cooper, Courtney Ryley. "Easy Come, Easy Go: As Told by Poker Alice Tubbs to Courtney Ryley Cooper." *Saturday Evening Post*, December 3, 1927.

Creede Pioneer Society of Denver Collection, MSS.170, History Colorado, Denver, Colorado.

DeArment, Robert K. *Bat Masterson: The Man and the Legend*. Norman: University of Oklahoma Press, 1979.

Donovan, Dave. "Ye Olde Curiosity Shop: A Philosophical Ghost Story." The Distributist, November 3, 2016. https://datadistributist.wordpress.com.

Feitz, Leland. *A Quick History of Creede: Colorado Boom Town*. 13th Printing. Colorado Springs: Little London Press, 1969.

———. *Soapy Smith's Creede: "The Silver Camp in 1892."* Colorado Springs: Little London Press, 1973.

Harbert, Charles A. *Creede, Colorado History…Insights and Views through Postcards and Photographs.* Wellington, CO: Vestige Press, 2010.

History Colorado. "Rio Grande Hotel." www.historycolorado.org.

Horn, Jonathon C. "Brunot Agreement." *Colorado Encyclopedia,* https://coloradoencyclopedia.org/article/brunot-agreement.

Jacobs, Janis. *Ribs of Silver Hearts of Gold.* Vol. 2. Creede, CO: Creede Historical Society, 1994.

LaFont, John. *58 Years Around Creede.* Alamosa, CO: Sangre de Cristo Printing, 1971.

———. *Homesteaders of the Upper Rio Grande.* Birmingham, AL: Oxmoor Press, 1971.

Mackall, Jan. *Brothels, Bordellos, & Bad Girls: Prostitution in Colorado, 1860–1930.* Albuquerque: University of New Mexico Press, 2004.

———. *Red Light Women of the Rocky Mountains.* Albuquerque: University of New Mexico Press, 2009.

Mumey, Nolie. *Creede: The History of a Colorado Silver Mining Town.* Denver: Artcraft Press, 1949.

Smith, Jeff. *Alias Soapy Smith: The Life and Death of a Scoundrel.* Juneau, AK: Klondike Research, 2009.

Todd, Mark, and Kym O'Connell-Todd. *Wild West Ghosts: An Amateur Ghost Hunting Guide for Haunted Hotels in Southwest Colorado.* Gunnison, CO: Raspberry Creek Books, Ltd., 2015.

Wagner, Sandra, and Carol Ann Wetherill. *Hidden History of the Upper Rio Grande.* Charleston: The History Press, 2017.

Warman, Cy. *The Prospector: Story of the Life of Nicholas C. Creede.* Denver: Great Divide Publishing, 1894.

Williams, Nancy. *Haunted Hotels of Southern Colorado.* Charleston, SC: The History Press, 2019.

Wolle, Muriel Sibell. *Stampede to Timberline: The Ghost Towns and Mining Camps of Colorado.* 2nd ed. Chicago: Swallow Press, 1974.

Ye Olde Curiosity Shop. "Sylvester." https://yeoldecuriosityshop.com.

Newspapers

Alamosa Courier
Alamosa Journal
Aspen Daily Leader
Aspen Daily Times
Boulder Daily Camera
Colorado Daily Chieftain
Creede Candle
Creede Chronicle
Gunnison Daily News-Democrat
Herald Democrat
Littleton Independent
Mineral County Miner
Rocky Mountain News
Saguache Crescent
Salida Mail
San Juan Prospector
Silver Thread Summer Guide
Steamboat Pilot

ABOUT THE AUTHOR

Kandra Payne is a native of Creede, Colorado, and holds a degree in drama from Colorado College. She worked six seasons at the Creede Repertory Theatre before becoming an Equity Stage Manager, and she has lived and worked in most of the great cities of this country including, Chicago, Seattle, New York, Washington, D.C., and Los Angeles. She now resides in Santa Fe, New Mexico, with her husband and daughter and is happy to be only a stone's throw from Creede. In the winter, you'll find her working deep among the stacks at the Santa Fe Public Library, and in the summer, she's home in Creede telling ghost stories to just about anyone who will listen.

Visit us at
www.historypress.com